Traditional
CAPE
MALAY
Cooking

Traditional
CAPE
MALAY
Cooking

ZAINAB LAGARDIEN

This edition published in 2008 by Struik Publishers
(a member of New Holland Publishing (Pty) Ltd)
New Holland Publishing is a member of Avusa Ltd
Cornelis Struik House, 80 McKenzie Street, Cape town 8001
86–88 Edgware Road, London, W2 2EA, United Kingdom
Unit 1, 66 Gibbes Street, Chatswood, NSW 2067, Australia
218 Lake Road, Northcote, Auckland, New Zealand

www.struik.co.za

Originally published as
Everyday Cape Malay Cooking 1995, 1998

1 2 3 4 5 6 7 8 9 10

Copyright © in text: Zainab Lagardien 1995, 1998, 2008
Copyright © in published edition:
Struik Publishers (Pty) Ltd 2008

PUBLISHER'S NOTE
Please note that all cup measurements are approximate.

EDITORS Glynne Williamson (1998) and Irma van Wyk (2008)
DESIGNER Janine Damon and Helen Henn
COVER CONCEPT Beverley Dodd
STYLIST Macushla Falkiner
FOOD PREPARATION Ivy Tingwe and Zainab Lagardien
PHOTOGRAPHERS All images by Alain Proust except for the
following: Lanz von Hörsten/Images of Africa: pages 2–3;
Keith Young/Images of Africa: pages 10–11, 20–21, 28–29, 38–39,
48–49, 62–63, 76–77, 90–91, 110–111, 120–121, 134–135
Ridwaan Mohamed: pages 100–101

PROPS Go East, Past Tunes, Hans Niehaus Collectors' Specialist,
The Colonial Cotton Company, Collector's Corner Antiques,
The Junk Shop, Peter Visser Interiors, Stuttafords, Garlicks,
The Yellow Door, House & Interiors at Bric-a-Brac Lane

Reproduction by Hirt & Carter Cape (Pty) Ltd

ISBN 978-1-77007-671-6

IMAGES OF AFRICA
PHOTO LIBRARY

Over 40 000 unique African images available to purchase from
our image bank at www.imagesofafrica.co.za

CONTENTS

INTRODUCTION

ACKNOWLEDGEMENTS

I dedicate this book to my son, Bienjamien, who becomes very noisy when he cooks for a family wedding!

I wish to thank the Struik Publishing Group for accepting my manuscript and making a dream come true, especially publishing manager Linda de Villiers, designer Odette Marais and editor Glynne Williamson, who spent many hours in my kitchen learning our ways.

I also wish to give credit to the photographer Alain Proust, stylist Macushla Falkiner and my co-chef Ivy Tingwe for their professionalism.

I would also like to thank my family and friends for their support and encouragement in helping me compile this book, thereby preserving our traditions:

My sister Fatima Abdul, also a caterer, for assisting with the catering ideas;

My daughters (née Solomon) Lutfeyah Jacobs, Mariam Tyers, Rashieda Isaacs and Noohr Samodien;

My granddaughters, Ruweyda Jacobs for copy typing, Shanaaz Tyers for typing all the fish dishes and Zyreena Tyers, my assistant who plays an important role in the catering; and also to Nazley Gaidien for co-ordinating the typists, and her daughters Shanaaz and Amina Gaidien;

Fatima Du Preez, Mymoena Dollie and Rowlda Booley for also helping with the typing;

Special thanks to my only son Bienjamien Solomon, a bulk cooker himself, for giving me moral support – with his wife, his four sisters and my granddaughters, he could cater for and co-ordinate any large function;

Lastly to my children's late father, Abdul Azeze Solomon, who inspired and encouraged me to put this book together.

A WORD FROM THE AUTHOR

I was born (Bis'millah) at no. 14 Godfrey Street off Hanover Street in District Six. I was only six years old when my mother and the baby were laid to rest and I went to live with my grandmother. She was a well-known konfyt-maker, catering for special functions, and life with her was a very colourful one. She reared us on home-made breads and konfyts, so the introduction to cooking for my sister and me began at an early age!

First we learnt about fruit. To make konfyt, pieces of fig were nipped off in tiny spots, grated or cut with a cross at the bottom and lowered into salt water overnight. Oranges were done in the same way, with pips and pith removed. Then we learnt about fish. Snoek was salted and hung under a muslin cloth to dry in the wind. Before sunset it was strung up in the fireplace. Pounded snoek biltong with a pinch of fine chilli is still a family favourite, served with 'boeretroos' black coffee.

My grandmother made up for everything I'd lost in my mother, my aunts also helping with my culinary education. Aunty Fatima always iced the family biscuits, cakes and puddings, and also taught handicrafts. I was taught to decorate biscuits, then moved on to making quick smoortjies. Special lessons were given on cooking and braising meats or making fish meals. Once I'd mastered these, my love for cooking, baking and brewing developed. The kitchen was, and still is, a busy place and the best place to be. Gradually my cooking and baking improved and I eventually went into bulk cooking for special occasions and catering in hotels. By the time I left the hotel kitchens I'd become quite an expert – I'd enjoyed the challenges I'd put to myself and the experience has proved invaluable.

As a child I can remember breads being baked at the bakery for 2 pence a loaf. The bakery was opposite the wash-house where washing was done for 6 pence. Pickled snoek cost only 4 pence a piece (about 500 g folded double, ready to be steamed, flaked or smoored in a variety of ways). Mutton was sold for 6 pence a piece (about 500 g). Things have changed a bit since then!

Malay cooking can vary from tangy to moderately hot. The recipes in this book are not highly spiced and can be seasoned according to taste. Starseed petal (star anise) is the ingredient that I use to add a special flavour to many of my savoury dishes.

I hope that you and your family will enjoy these recipes that have been gathered over many years and form part of our rich heritage. Insh'allah!

Clockwise from top left: fresh root ginger, green and red chillies, curry powder, sesame seeds, turmeric, fresh dhania leaves

Allspice

These are small, unripe, sun-dried berries of the pimento tree. The flavour is a combination of cinnamon, nutmeg and cloves, and is used in curries, soups, bredies, desserts and cakes.

Aniseed

The seeds of the anise plant have a sweet, pungent flavour which is similar to liquorice, and are mainly used in confectionery.

Atjar

Atjar is a relish made from sliced vegetables or fruit, flavoured with spices and covered with vinegar or oil.

Barishap

This is the Malay name for fennel seeds, which have a slightly bitter aniseed flavour. Ground barishap is used in breyanis or fish dishes.

Bay leaf

Bay leaves come from the evergreen bay or laurel tree, and are used to flavour meat dishes, pickled fish, soups and bredies. They have a slightly bitter taste and must be discarded before the meal is served.

Bobotie

This is a favourite Malay dish, made of curried mince or fish baked slowly in the oven with a beaten egg poured over it. Bobotie is always served with rice.

Bredie

A type of stew, the flavour is determined by the kind of vegetable added. Onions are browned in oil or fat, then meat (usually mutton or lamb) is added and braised over a low heat. Vegetables are added last and braised on top of the meat.

Breyani

This is a semi-dry dish consisting of rice, spices and meat, chicken, fish, lentils or eggs, served in one pot.

Cardamom

Cardamom is a member of the ginger family, and is also known as the Seed of Paradise. It is sold ground or whole, and is used to flavour curries, soups, eggs, salads, meat, breyanis, puddings and cakes.

Chilli

Fresh chillies must be used sparingly, dried chilli more freely. Dried and powdered chillies are known as red or cayenne pepper. Green chillies have more flavour and are juicier, but the red chillies are hotter. Chillies are used to flavour curry dishes, chutneys and sambals.

Cinnamon

Cinnamon comes from the bark of a tropical tree which is rolled into cinnamon sticks or powdered. The lighter-brown type is known as cinnamon. The reddish-brown cinnamon is called cassia. Cinnamon has a sweet flavour, a strong, spicy aroma and is used to flavour various drinks, and savoury and sweet dishes.

Cloves

Cloves are unopened buds of the myrtaceous tree, which are picked when they turn red and then sun-dried. Ground cloves are stronger than whole ones. They are used as a pungent, fragrant spice to flavour a variety of savoury and sweet dishes.

Curry

Malay curry is slightly sweeter than Indian curry with less chilli and more spices. It is usually eaten with rice or rotis, accompanied by sambals.

Curry leaves

These can be bought fresh or dried. Fresh ones are used to garnish curry meals. Dried ones add extra flavour to savoury dishes.

Curry powder

This is a mixture of spices and consists of cayenne pepper, coriander, cumin seed, fenugreek, turmeric, cinnamon, cardamom, cloves, fennel, ginger, mace, mustard and black or white pepper.

Dhal

Dhal is an Indian lentil often used in breyanis.

Dhania

Fresh coriander leaves, or dhania, are used to garnish curries or to add flavour to savoury dishes. It is also available in powdered form.

Eid

Two Eids are celebrated during the year – Eidul-Fitr (the Festival of Charity) and Eidul-Adgha (the Festival of Sacrifice). Eidul-Fitr takes place the day after Ramadan and is often referred to as Labarang. Eidul-Adgha takes place 70 days after Ramadan.

Garlic

This is a bulbous plant, smaller than an onion, with a strong taste. It can be used fresh or dried to flavour savoury dishes and is often used together with fresh root ginger.

Masala

This is a mixture of certain spices, used in breyanis, curries, atjars and other savoury dishes. There are many different varieties of masala, including red leaf (which contains more ground chilli powder), leaf and tandoori masala.

Kabob

A kabob is a hard-boiled egg wrapped in mince meat and fried in fat or oil.

Labarang

Refer to entry under 'Eid'.

Methi

Methi, or fenugreek, is the pod of an annual plant related to the pea. The seed is finely ground and mixed with curry powder to flavour rice, atjars and vegetable dishes.

Mint

Mint is a fresh-tasting herb with a strong flavour that must be used sparingly.

Mustard seed

This is a small, dark seed used to flavour atjars, pickles and savoury dishes.

Naartjie peel

Naartjie peel is dried, ground into a powder and stored in a jar to flavour cakes, puddings, meat dishes and vegetables. It goes well with cardamom and cinnamon.

Nutmeg

Nutmeg comes from the seeds of the fruit of an evergreen tree. The dried membrane that surrounds the fruit is called mace. Nutmeg is used to flavour bredies and confectionery.

Pepper

Black and white pepper come from a vine that bears small berries. When picked just before ripening, they yield black pepper. Ripe berries are sun-dried and ground to form white pepper.

Rosewater

The essence from rose petals is used to flavour puddings and milk drinks.

Ramadan

This is the ninth month of the Muslim year during which strict fasting occurs, starting before sunrise and ending at sunset. This most important of all fasts ends after 30 days when the new moon has been sighted.

Roti

Roti is the Malay word for unleavened bread adapted from the Indian recipe. Rotis are often served unbuttered with curries instead of rice and used to scoop up the curry in place of cutlery.

Saffron

Saffron is a rare and expensive spice made from the stamens of the wild crocus. It is used to tint and flavour savoury dishes.

Sambal

Of Javanese origin, a sambal is a tangy condiment, made from grated vegetables or fruit, salted and flavoured with vinegar and chillies. It is usually served with curries or bredies.

Smoor

Smoor can be translated to mean braised. Vegetables and meat can be smoored together in oil or fat.

Starseed petal

This is also called star anise because of its star shape. The seeds have a tangy flavour and are used whole or ground in savoury dishes.

Tamarind

This is the fruit of a tropical tree with a sweetish-sour flavour. The fruit is boiled or is sometimes sucked raw for the taste. The pods are pulped, boiling water is poured over a lump of tamarind and left to soak for a short while, resulting in tamarind water. This liquid is used to flavour curries.

Turmeric

Turmeric comes from a perennial tropical plant and is a member of the ginger family. The root is dried and ground, and used to colour curry and rice and flavour savoury dishes. It is sometimes called 'borrie'.

Clockwise from top left: starseed petal, fresh garlic, cardamom, cinnamon, allspice, cloves

CHAPTER 1

SOUPS AND LIGHT MEALS

Soups, nourishing and tasty, are a popular winter meal and are often served during the fast of Ramadan. Some of the light meals can also be served as snacks or as accompaniments to a delicious feast!

SPLIT PEA AND DUMPLING SOUP

Subtly spiced pea soup with dumplings makes a filling lunch-time meal.

½ kg stewing beef
2 pieces sheep shin
1 medium onion, chopped
about 2 litres (8 cups) boiling water
500 g (2½ cups) dried split peas, soaked overnight in boiling water
10 ml (2 tsp) medium-coarse salt
1 tomato, blanched, peeled and pulped
3 young carrots, scraped
2 large potatoes, peeled and halved
10 ml (2 tsp) tomato paste
3 whole cloves
4 allspice
1 starseed petal (star anise)
5 ml (1 tsp) white sugar
125 ml (½ cup) chopped parsley
125 ml (½ cup) chopped celery

DUMPLINGS
250 ml (1 cup) self-raising flour
10 ml (2 tsp) melted butter
a pinch ground nutmeg

In a deep pot on medium heat scorch the meat and onion. Pour the boiling water onto the meat and add the remaining soup ingredients, except the parsley and celery. Cook the soup for about 50 minutes. Remove the carrots and potatoes, mash them and return to the pot. Reduce the heat and add the parsley and celery. Make a thick dough by mixing the flour, butter and nutmeg with a little liquid from the soup. Dipping a dessertspoon into the pot and then into the dough prevents the dough sticking to the spoon. Drop spoonfuls of dough into the soup to make dumplings. After 10 minutes remove from the heat and serve.
Serves 6

MASALA FRIED SNOEK ROE

500 ml (2 cups) oil
1 kg snoek roe, washed and dried
5 ml (1 tsp) salt
5 ml (1 tsp) red masala
2 cardamom pods, lightly crushed

Heat the oil in a saucepan over medium heat. While the oil is heating, marinate the roe with salt and masala. Add the cardamom pods to the oil. Slice the roe and add, taking care not to crowd the saucepan. After 5 minutes, reduce the heat to low. Continue until all the roes are cooked and golden brown. Drain the roes, reserving the oil, and serve with chips.
Serves 8

OLD CAPE CREAM OF TOMATO SOUP

This recipe won me first prize in a Cape Argus cookery competition a few years ago.

Old Cape Cream of Tomato Soup

500 g fresh ripe tomatoes
175 ml (¾ cup) red lentils
1 kg sheep knuckles
3 marrow bones
1 medium onion, finely chopped
3 litres (12 cups) boiling water
1 large turnip or potato,
    peeled and cubed
4 medium carrots, peeled
    and cubed
15 ml (1 tbsp) tomato paste
5 allspice
5 whole cloves
10 ml (2 tsp) sugar
125 ml (½ cup) chopped parsley
125 ml (½ cup) chopped celery
5 ml (1 tsp) black or white pepper
a pinch turmeric
fresh cream for serving

Blanch the tomatoes, then peel and chop. Soak the lentils in lukewarm water for about 30 minutes and set aside. Soak the meat and bones in lukewarm water for about 5 minutes and set aside. Rinse the meat and bones twice. Heat a deep, heavy-based cooking pot on medium heat. Transfer the meat and bones to the pot and top with the onion. Scorch the meat slightly, but do not braise. Add 2 litres (8 cups) of boiling water and leave to cook for about 1½ hours, stirring occasionally. Add the turnip or potato and carrots, and the rest of ingredients except the parsley, celery, pepper and turmeric. Cook for about 30 minutes. During the cooking process, remove any scum that may form on the surface. Add the parsley and celery, and cook slowly for 30 minutes before serving time. Add the pepper and turmeric and stir well. Serve with a tablespoon of cream swirled into each bowl.
Serves 8

COUNTRY-STYLE BUNNY CHOW

The 'bunny' represents the loaf, supposedly the size of a rabbit, and 'chow' is a Durban-Indian word for filling.

CHOW
15 ml (1 tbsp) oil
1 onion, chopped
250 g tenderised steak, cubed
250 ml (1 cup) water
2.5 ml (½ tsp) turmeric
2.5 ml (½ tsp) masala
2.5 ml (½ tsp) salt
1 piece stick cinnamon
10 ml (2 tsp) tomato sauce
2.5 ml (½ tsp) garlic and
 ginger paste

2.5 ml (½ tsp) ground jeera (cumin)
3 slices red pepper
1 x 410 g tin butter beans, drained

BUNNY
2 small, oval loaves or
 short French loaves

Heat the oil over medium heat, add the onion and scorch. Add the steak and water, steam until the water has cooked away, then stir-fry until the meat is just tender. Add the remaining ingredients, taking care to add the beans last. Slice off a quarter of the loaf lengthwise, scoop out some of the bread and fill with the chow. No cutlery needed here!
Serves 2

Country-Style Bunny Chow

BARLEY SOUP

A favourite, well-tried soup with an added tang of starseed petal.

500 g neck of mutton
2 marrow bones
500 g mutton knuckles
375 ml (1½ cups) barley
1 onion, chopped
3 litres (12 cups) boiling water
3 carrots, peeled and cubed
1 turnip or potato, peeled and cubed
and soaked in cold water
2 soft, red tomatoes,
blanched, peeled and pulped
6 allspice
4 whole cloves
1 starseed petal (star anise)

15 ml (1 tbsp) salt
15 ml (1 tbsp) tomato paste
5 ml (1 tsp) white pepper
125 ml (½ cup) chopped parsley
125 ml (½ cup) chopped celery

Soak the meat for about 5 minutes and the barley for about 1 hour separately in lukewarm water. Drain the meat. Heat a saucepan on medium heat and add the meat and onion. Allow to scorch a little. Pour over 1 litre (4 cups) boiling water and raise the temperature to high. Add the remaining 2 litres (8 cups) boiling water. Drain the barley and add to saucepan with the remaining ingredients except the pepper, parsley and celery. Cook rapidly for 1 hour, removing any scum that may form but taking care not to discard the spices. Reduce the heat to low and add the remaining ingredients. Simmer for a further 30 minutes.
Serves 6

FARM-STYLE SOUP

Chunky and hearty, this soup is perfect for a cold winter's night!

15 ml (1 tbsp) oil
3 slices beef shin
2 marrow bones or 1 kg mutton knuckles
1 medium onion, chopped
3 litres (12 cups) boiling water
4 young carrots, peeled and cubed
500 g tomatoes, blanched and peeled
1 x 410 g tin whole-kernel corn
½ small spitskop cabbage
(curly top), finely grated
4 whole cloves
6 allspice
15 ml (1 tbsp) tomato paste
10 ml (2 tsp) sugar

10 ml (2 tsp) salt
2.5 ml (½ tsp) turmeric
1 x 410 g tin baked beans
125 ml (½ cup) chopped parsley
125 ml (½ cup) chopped celery
10 ml (2 tsp) ground black pepper

This soup will take 2 hours to cook in a saucepan or 20 minutes in a pressure cooker. Heat the oil in a saucepan and scorch the meat and onions, but do not braise. Add 2 litres (8 cups) boiling water to the saucepan. Add the remaining ingredients, except the baked beans, celery, parsley and pepper, and cook rapidly for 2 hours, removing any scum that may form. Return to the saucepan any spices that were scooped up in the process. Now add 1 litre (4 cups) boiling water and turn the heat to low. Add the remaining ingredients, except the beans, and simmer until the meat is tender and the vegetables are cooked. Add the beans 5 minutes before serving.
Serves 6

NOTE: The flavour of the soup is not complete without adding marrow bones to the soup during cooking.

BAKED BEAN SOUP

500 g stewing beef, cubed
2 marrow bones
1 medium onion, chopped
2 litres (8 cups) boiling water
20 ml (1½ tbsp) tomato paste
1 small tomato, blanched, peeled and chopped
1 turnip or potato, peeled and diced
4 medium carrots, peeled and diced
60 ml (¼ cup) chopped celery
1 starseed petal (star anise)
5 allspice
5 whole cloves
1 x 410 g tin baked beans
5 ml (1 tsp) pepper
60 ml (¼ cup) chopped parsley

Heat a saucepan on medium heat and add the meat and marrow bones. Add the chopped onion to the meat and scorch until lightly browned – do not allow to braise. Now add the boiling water and remaining ingredients except the baked beans, pepper and parsley. Cook for about 40 minutes. Remove any scum that may form on the surface, taking care not to discard the spices. Add the baked beans, pepper and parsley 10 minutes before serving.
Serves 4–5

DHALTJIES

The Malay word for chilli bites is dhaltjies.

375 ml (1½ cups) pea flour or Chilli Bite Mix
175 ml (¾ cup) self-raising flour
½ bunch spinach leaves, torn into small pieces
5 ml (1 tsp) salt
5 ml (1 tsp) turmeric
2.5 ml (½ tsp) red masala
60 g (¼ cup) fresh ginger
1 green chilli, chopped or 2.5 ml (½ tsp) crushed chillies
1 small onion, finely chopped
1 slice red pepper, finely chopped
5 ml (1 tsp) ground jeera (cumin)
30 ml (2 tbsp) butter, melted
5 ml (1 tsp) baking powder
about 250 ml (1 cup) water
375 ml (1½ cups) oil for deep-frying

Mix all the ingredients together, except the oil, to make a fairly stiff batter – it must be manageable but not runny. Heat the oil in a deep pan on medium heat until warm but not hot. Dip a dessertspoon into the oil, then into the mixture (this prevents the batter from sticking to the spoon), and drop spoonfuls of batter into the oil. Fry slowly until golden-brown and crisp. Make sure that the oil doesn't get too hot during frying. Pierce with a fork to test if they are cooked – if the fork is dry, the dhaltjies are ready. Remove from the pan and allow to drain on kitchen paper or in a colander. Serve immediately as a snack or starter.
Makes about 30, depending on size

NOTE: Dhaltjies can be frozen if dried chillis have been used. Freeze them wrapped in foil or in an airtight container. If using Chilli Bite Mix, test the batter before adding salt, as it already contains salt.

SAMOOSAS

Of Indian origin, these piquant pastry triangles are time-consuming to make but the results are worth the effort. Samoosa pastry is known as pur.

4 x 250 ml (4 cups) cake flour
5 ml (1 tsp) turmeric
5 ml (1 tsp) salt
375 ml (1½ cups) lukewarm water
10 ml (2 tsp) oil
500 g steak mince
2.5 ml (½ tsp) cayenne pepper
1 green chilli or a pinch cayenne pepper
a pinch jeera (cumin) seeds
a pinch leaf masala
1 medium onion, chopped
oil for deep-frying

Form a soft dough with the flour, a pinch turmeric, salt and water. Leave to stand. Heat the oil in a saucepan. Stir-fry the meat with all the remaining ingredients except onion. Stir until dry and remove from the heat. Pour a little boiling water on the onion, leave for a few minutes and strain.

Spoon into a clean cloth and twist the cloth tightly to extract excess the liquid and strong flavour of the onion. Add to the meat and mix well. The filling must be dryish or it will escape from the pastry during cooking.

Sprinkle a little flour onto a table or board. Break off balls of dough, the size of eggs – keep the hands and rolling pin well-floured – and roll out four of the balls as thinly as possible into four circles. Smear the dough circles with a little oil, especially the edges. Lightly sprinkle some flour round the edges and middle. Repeat the process until you have a stack of four circles. Do not oil the top or the bottom circle. Roll out the stacked circles into one large, thin circle and cut the sides evenly to form a square. Place the pastry on an ungreased baking sheet or roti griddle. Parbake at 100 °C for 2–3 minutes. When the leaves show signs of loosening, remove from the baking sheet. With a sharp knife, cut into 14 cm x 6 cm strips. Separate the layers. Cover with a damp cloth to prevent the pastry from drying out. Hold a strip of pastry in one hand and pull the bottom corner across. Fold upwards to form a triangle with sharp corners and a pocket, and fill with the mince mixture. Fold the pastry across the top of the triangle to seal. Make a thick paste with 60 ml (¼ cup) flour and a little cold water. Use this paste to stick the ends together after filling. The filling will escape during cooking if the samoosa is not folded down well. Deep-fry in hot oil over medium heat, turning once or twice until golden brown. Remove from the pan with a slotted spoon and drain on absorbent paper.

Makes about 24 samoosas

NOTE: Samoosas can be frozen, but for no longer than 6 months and can be deep-fried immediately without defrosting. Leftover pur can be deep-fried slowly in hot oil.

Samoosas and dhaltjies

FISH CAKES

A favourite weekday meal that's quick and economical to make.

1 x 410 g tin middlecut or
extra-large plain pilchards
1 small onion
4 cloves garlic
60 ml (¼ cup) parsley or
6 mint leaves, chopped
4 slices stale white bread, soaked in
water for 5 minutes and squeezed dry
a pinch turmeric
a pinch grated nutmeg
1 egg, lightly beaten
5 ml (1 tsp) butter
a pinch salt
1 green pepper, chopped
oil for frying

Drain the fish, remove the centre bones and place in a mixing bowl. Chop the onion, garlic and parsley separately – the parsley should be finer than the onion, and the garlic much finer than the parsley – and add to the fish. Add the bread and mix together. Add the remaining ingredients and mix lightly. Wet your hands in a small bowl of cold water before forming small round fish cakes. Fry in not-too-deep oil over medium heat. For crispy fish cakes, turn a colander upside-down over the pan while frying. Serve with cooked white rice, adding 2 small pieces of stick cinnamon and a pinch of turmeric for extra flavour and colour. Chutney on the side rounds off the meal.
Serves 5

SNOEK ROE SMOORTJIE

Serve with fresh rolls as a light lunch.

60 ml (¼ cup) oil drained from
Masala Fried Snoek Roe (page 12)
1 small onion, chopped
3 tomatoes, blanched, peeled
and pulped
a pinch salt
10 ml (2 tsp) sugar
6 slices red or green pepper
6 snoek roes, washed and
slightly dried

Heat the oil in a saucepan, toss in the onion and braise until golden brown. Add the tomato. Keep the heat on medium and braise the onion and tomato. Now add the salt, sugar and sliced pepper. Cut the roes into portions, add to the saucepan and simmer for 10 minutes. Serve immediately.
Serves 5

PICKLED KABELJOU

Pickled fish is traditionally served over the festive season.

1 medium kabeljou, sliced
15 ml (1 tbsp) salt
10 ml (2 tsp) red leaf masala
185 ml (¾ cup) oil
2 cardamom pods, split open
375 ml (1½ cups) malt vinegar
10 ml (2 tsp) turmeric
15 ml (1 tbsp) sugar
2 medium onions, sliced into rings
250 ml (1 cup) water
1 bay leaf
4 allspice
1 whole clove

Wash the fish and marinate in 5 ml (1 tsp) salt and 2.5 ml (½ tsp) masala for about 2 minutes. Heat the pan, add the oil and cardamom, and fry the fish in shallow oil until light brown. Spread the fish in a large, shallow glass dish. Set aside. Heat the saucepan and add the vinegar, turmeric, sugar, remaining salt and masala, onion rings and water. Bring to the boil and remove from the heat. Toss in the bay leaf and spices, cover and leave to cool slightly. When lukewarm, pour the mixture over the fish, ensuring that the fish is completely covered. For the best results, store, covered, in a glass dish for 24 hours to allow the flavours to develop.

Serves 4

Pickled kabeljou

CHAPTER 2

FISH AND SEAFOOD

The Cape Malays have had fishermen in their families
for generations, and fish, served in a variety of dishes, has
become a favourite item on the menu. Snoek is particularly
popular and is prepared in almost any way imaginable!

OVEN SNOEK

The ingredients used in this traditional Malay fish dish enhance the special flavour of the snoek.

Oven Snoek

1 medium, freshly caught snoek
10 ml (2 tsp) coarse salt
5 ml (1 tsp) red masala
45 ml (3 tbsp) melted butter
  or margarine
a few tomato slices
a few onion rings

Remove the head and tail of the fish
and set these pieces aside. Wash the
remainder of the fish well and salt. Cut the
side bone to allow the salt to soak into
the fish, leave to stand for a few minutes,
then dust with masala. Preheat the oven
to 200°C. Grease a roasting pan lightly
with a little of the butter. Place the fish in
the pan and top with the remaining butter,
the tomato slices and onion rings. Bake
the snoek for about 25 minutes or until
the fish is cooked. Serve with Light Brown
Rolls (page 138) and Chilli Sauce (page 92)
or Apricot and Peach Chutney (page 99).
Serves 6

NOTES:
- Make a smoor with the head and tail
  of the fish from the Oven Snoek recipe
  by steaming them with salt, onion and
  ground black pepper. Alternatively, use
  the Old Cape Smoorsnoek recipe on
  the opposite page.
- Instead of using peas in the Old Cape
  Smoorsnoek recipe (opposite), add a
  shredded spitskop (curly top) cabbage
  and a pinch of turmeric.

OLD CAPE SMOORSNOEK

Smoorsnoek is popular amongst the Malay community – this is one of my favourite versions.

60 ml (¼ cup) oil
1 onion, chopped
500 g salted, dried snoek,
steamed and shredded
5 ml (1 tsp) sugar
1 red or green chilli, chopped
1 x 410 g tin peas or
410 g frozen peas

Heat the oil in a broad, shallow saucepan, toss in the chopped onion and braise. Add the steamed and shredded snoek, sugar, chilli and peas. Reduce heat to low for 5 minutes, then remove from heat and serve with white rice and Apricot and Peach Chutney (page 99).

Serves 4

CRISPY SILVERFISH

The silverfish is a soft, moist and tasty fish, and is flavoured here with garlic, turmeric and masala.

2 small, freshly caught silverfish,
scaled and gutted
10 ml (2 tsp) salt
5 ml (1 tsp) turmeric
5 ml (1 tsp) roasted red masala
3 cloves garlic, crushed
125 ml (½ cup) oil
60 ml (¼ cup) flour for coating

Mix the spices together and marinate the fish for a few minutes in a glass or porcelain dish. Heat the oil in a heavy-based pan over medium heat. Coat fish lightly with flour and transfer to a pan. Fry each side until done. Serve on a platter with Long-grain White Rice (page 81). Stir-fried onions and Braised Tomato (page 78) are good accompaniments.

Serves 3

TANGY PILCHARD SMOOR

An economical, weekday meal.

60 ml (¼ cup) oil
3 pieces stick cinnamon
1 large onion, chopped
15 ml (1 tbsp) tomato sauce
250 ml (1 cup) water
a pinch turmeric
5 ml (1 tsp) leaf masala
8 curry leaves
a pinch salt
a pinch sugar
1 starseed petal (star anise)
1 x 410 g tin plain pilchards, drained
and middle bone removed

Heat the oil and cinnamon in a saucepan. Add the onion and braise lightly. Add remaining ingredients, cover the saucepan and cook for a few minutes to allow the flavour to develop. Turn off the heat. It is now ready to serve with white rice.

Serves 5

KABELJOU TOMATO SMOOR

The kabeljou (named from the Dutch 'kabeljauw') is complemented by the tomato smoor.

1 small kabeljou, sliced
375 ml (1½ cups) oil
10 ml (2 tsp) cake flour

MARINADE
10 ml (2 tsp) salt
3.5 ml (½ tsp) leaf masala
4 cloves garlic, crushed

SMOOR
30 ml (2 tbsp) oil
1 medium onion,
thinly sliced
250 g (1 cup) tomatoes, diced
2.5 ml (½ tsp) salt
10 ml (2 tsp) sugar
3 slices green pepper
a pinch masala

Wash and drain the fish. Mix the marinade ingredients together and rub into the fish. Leave to marinate for a few minutes. To make the smoor, heat the oil in a pan, add the onion and braise until lightly browned. Add the tomatoes, salt, sugar and sliced pepper, and cook for 10 minutes over low heat. Remove from the heat and add masala. Set aside and keep warm. Heat the oil in a heavy-based pan on medium-high. Dust the fish lightly on both sides with flour and place in pan. (Dusting the fish with flour prevents the flesh from breaking up and also gives it a golden colour.) Cover with a lid and cook, turning when golden-brown. Serve the fish and tomato smoor with Savoury Rice (page 80).

Serves 5

NOTE: Use Hottentot instead of kabeljou.

CAPE SALMON SMOOR

If Cape salmon is unavailable, use soldaat (santa) instead.

7.5 ml (1½ tsp) salt
5 ml (1 tsp) leaf masala
1.5 kg Cape salmon cutlets
250 ml (1 cup) oil
1 large onion, chopped
1 small tomato, blanched, peeled
and pulped
4 potatoes, peeled and cubed
500 ml (2 cups) water
10 ml (2 tsp) salt
½ red or green pepper, sliced
1 small green chilli, halved
1 starseed petal (star anise)

Mix 7.5 ml salt (1½ tsp) and masala together, rub into the fish and allow to marinate for 10 minutes. Heat 125 ml (½ cup) oil in a pan and fry fish lightly for 5 minutes on each side. Remove from the pan and set aside. Use the same pan and the remaining 125 ml (½ cup) oil to make the smoor. Heat the oil on medium heat and, when warm, but not too hot, toss in the onion and braise until golden brown. Stir occasionally. Now add the tomato and potatoes with 375 ml (1½ cups) cold water and 2.5 ml (½ tsp) salt. Cook for about 10 minutes. Reduce the heat and add fish and remaining ingredients. Add the remaining 125 ml (½ cup) cold water and simmer gently. When done, serve with Braised Brown Rice (page 81) and Chilli Sauce (page 92).

Serves 5

FISH BOBOTIE

A simply delicious dish! Any type of firm white fish can be used.

500 g hake steaks
10 ml (2 tsp) chopped parsley
6 fresh mint leaves, chopped
3 cloves garlic, crushed
10 ml (2 tsp) soft margarine
a pinch leaf masala
5 ml (1 tsp) salt
a pinch grated nutmeg
a pinch ground black pepper
1 small tomato, cubed
a pinch turmeric
1 small onion, chopped
4 slices stale bread, soaked in water for 5 minutes
2 eggs, lightly beaten

Steam the fish in a little water over medium heat for 10 minutes. Remove from heat and allow to cool. Flake fish and set aside. Mix remaining ingredients, except the 2 lightly beaten eggs, adding the bread last. Do not squeeze all the water out of the bread, otherwise the mixture will be too stiff. Add the fish to this mixture. Bake in the oven at 200 °C until light brown, then remove from the oven. Pour the beaten eggs over the fish mixture and return to the oven for a further 10 minutes or until it is browned on top. Serve immediately with chutney, Cinnamon Pumpkin (page 78) and mashed potatoes.
Serves 4

Fish Bobotie, served with Cinnamon Pumpkin (page 78)

MASALA STUMPNOSE

Kingklip, Cape salmon or snoek can be substituted for the stumpnose in this piquant dish.

1.5 kg white stumpnose
10 ml (2 tsp) salt
1 clove garlic, chopped
1 fresh green chilli, chopped or
2.5 ml (½ tsp) cayenne pepper
5 ml (1 tsp) leaf masala
5 ml (1 tsp) turmeric
1 lemon
375 ml (1½ cups) oil
2 cardamom pods, split open

Remove the fins from the fish and cut the fish into portions. Slit each portion at the top and salt the fish – the slits must be wide enough for the salt to soak in. Mix garlic, chilli or cayenne pepper, masala and turmeric together, then rub into the fish and allow to marinate for a few minutes. Watch out for sharp bones while marinating! Halve the lemon, remove the pips and squeeze the juice over the fish portions. Heat the oil and cardamom over medium heat and fry the fish, covered. Serve with Long-grain White Rice (page 81) and Cabbage, Carrot and Bean Atjar (page 98).
Serves 6

NOTE: Fish scales can easily be removed after soaking the fish in cold water for a while.

SHRIMP-Á-LA-TAIWAN

Shrimps are an extravagance but worth it.

125 ml (½ cup) oil
4 small pieces stick cinnamon
2 cardamom pods
1 large onion, chopped
1 small tomato, blanched,
peeled and pulped
15 ml (1 tbsp) tomato sauce
2 x 454 g packets peeled shrimps
5 ml (1 tsp) turmeric
5 ml (1 tsp) masala
12 curry leaves
¼ red or green pepper, chopped
5 ml (1 tsp) garlic and ginger paste
1 starseed petal (star anise)
7.5 ml (1½ tsp) salt
6 allspice
2 whole cloves
60 g (¼ cup) tamarind, soaked for
5 minutes in 125 ml (½ cup) boiling
water with 5 ml (1 tsp) sugar
5 ml (1 tsp) ground jeera (cumin)

Heat the oil in a heavy-based saucepan over medium heat. Add cinnamon and cardamom, then onion, and braise until golden brown. Add tomato and tomato sauce, and stir to mix thoroughly. Cook shrimps according to packet instructions. Add shrimps and the remaining ingredients, except the tamarind and jeera, to the onion mixture. Reduce the heat. Strain the tamarind through a sieve and, with the jeera, add the liquid to the mixture. Simmer gently for 5 minutes, stirring once or twice. Serve with Long-grain White Rice (page 81).
Serves 6

NOTE: Make sure you always buy whole fresh fish with bright, bulging eyes – never buy fish with dull eyes.

SMOORVIS AND BUTTER BEANS

Instead of soaking beans overnight, using tinned butter beans makes this a quick dish to prepare.

Smoorvis and Butter Beans

half a salted snoek
60 ml (¼ cup) oil
1 onion, sliced
**1 small tomato, blanched, peeled
and pulped**
5 ml (1 tsp) leaf masala
a pinch turmeric
1 cardamom pod
2 pieces stick cinnamon
a pinch ground jeera (cumin)
a pinch coriander
2 x 410 g tins butter beans, drained

Soak the snoek in cold water overnight. Rinse and steam in very little water. If you are in a hurry and don't have time for overnight soaking, pour a kettle of boiling water over the snoek, rinse and leave for a few minutes in a little cold water. Bone and flake the fish, then set aside. Heat the oil in a saucepan and braise the onion until golden-brown. Add the tomato and cook for a few minutes. Now mix the fish, then add the spices just before the fish is cooked. Simmer for a further 15 minutes before adding butter beans. Allow to heat through and serve with Long-grain White Rice (page 81).
Serves 4

TRAWLER'S FAVOURITE PANGHA

Pangha are firm, pinkish fish which are trawled all year round.

2 medium panghas
10 ml (2 tsp) salt
5 ml (1 tsp) leaf masala
4 cloves garlic, crushed
1 lemon, halved, pips removed
1 small green chilli, chopped
1 large onion, sliced
375 ml (1½ cups) oil
4 ripe tomatoes, cubed
1 starseed petal (star anise)
½ red or green pepper, sliced
10 ml (2 tsp) sugar
2 cardamom pods, split open

Clean and divide the fish into cutlets. As panghas' bones are very hard, chop off as much as possible. Wash the cutlets under slow-running cold water, then drain well. Mix 7.5 ml (1½ tsp) of the salt, the masala and garlic together. Add the juice of half the lemon and the chopped chilli. Pour over the cutlets and allow to marinate for a few minutes. Braise the onion in 15 ml (1 tbsp) of the oil in a light pan. Add the tomatoes, the remaining salt, starseed, pepper slices and sugar. Reduce the heat and cook for 10 minutes. If the tomatoes are very watery, cook a little longer, but don't let the mixture become too dry. Reduce the heat to medium and fry the fish in the remaining oil. Add one of the cardamom pods to the oil while frying the first batch of cutlets, and the other while frying the second batch. Enjoy this dish with Long-Grain White Rice (page 81) and tomato sauce or Chilli Sauce (page 92).
Serves 6

CHAPTER 3

POULTRY

Muslims do not eat pork, so poultry, meat and fish form part of their daily diet. Chicken and turkey dishes are often served during the Feast of Labarang (the Festival of Charity), while some are simply for everyday enjoyment.

CHICKEN PIE

The masala and cinnamon liven up an otherwise ordinary chicken pie. Serve with mashed potato and salads or vegetables.

FILLING
7.5 ml (1½ tsp) salt
5 ml (1 tsp) red masala
2 chicken drumsticks, deboned and each divided into three
2 chicken breasts, deboned and each divided into three
5 ml (1 tsp) margarine
2 small pieces stick cinnamon
15 ml (1 tbsp) oil or
10 ml (2 tsp) butter
1 small onion, chopped
4 small shreds green or red pepper
5 ml (1 tsp) red masala
2.5 ml (½ tsp) dried thyme
10 ml (2 tsp) cornflour made into a paste with water and a pinch salt

PASTRY
310 ml (1¼ cups) cake flour
125 ml (½ cup) self-raising flour
125 g (½ cup) butter
250 ml (1 cup) cold water
15 ml (1 tbsp) lemon juice
10 ml (2 tsp) oil
2.5 ml (½ tsp) salt
1 egg, beaten

Mix the salt and masala together, rub into the chicken pieces, and allow to marinate for a few minutes. Grill in a heavy-based saucepan in margarine on medium heat. Add the cinnamon and small quantities of water as the meat grills. Remove from the heat when cooked and set aside to cool. Heat the oil or butter in a pan and stir-fry the onion and pepper shreds. Add the remaining filling ingredients except the cornflour paste. When heated through, slowly stir in the cornflour paste for a few minutes. Remove from the heat.

To make the pastry, sift the flours together and lightly rub in the butter. Adding water a little at a time, add the remaining ingredients, except the egg, and form into a dough. Rest the dough for 15 minutes, roll out and divide in half. Line a round, ovenproof dish with half the pastry and bake blind for 5 minutes on the middle shelf at 200 °C. Remove from the oven and leave to cool. Spoon in the filling evenly. Place the other half of the pastry on top, press down and seal the overhanging edge. Cut off excess pastry, crimp the edges with a pastry cutter, and prick the top with a fork. Brush with the beaten egg before and after baking. Return to the oven and bake for 30 minutes.
Serves 4

JAVANESE CHICKEN

My ancestors come from Java and this delicious dish has been handed down from generation to generation.

3 small, fresh chickens, quartered
10 ml (2 tsp) medium-coarse salt
10 ml (2 tsp) red leaf masala
10 ml (2 tsp) peri-peri oil
175 g (¾ cup) margarine
6 pieces stick cinnamon
10–12 pineapple slices
1 kg medium potatoes, peeled and cut into chips
oil for deep-frying

Wash the chicken portions well and drain in a colander. Sprinkle the salt and masala on a smooth surface and rub the chicken into the mixture. Transfer to a large porcelain or glass bowl, and allow to marinate for a few minutes. Add the peri-peri oil, turn the chicken a few times and set aside for about 10 minutes. Heat a heavy-based saucepan or cast-iron roasting pan on medium heat and add the margarine. Add the chicken pieces and cinnamon. Allow to brown a little on one side before turning to brown the other side. Small amounts of water can be added as the chicken grills. Do not cover the pan. Fry the pineapple slices in a heavy-based pan over low heat in 15 ml (1 tbsp) chicken oil taken from the roasting pan. Deep-fry the potato chips and serve alongside the chicken. A favourite salad and fresh corn on the cob are perfect accompaniments.
Serves 10–12

MALAYAN CRUMBED CHICKEN

The chicken is steamed first, then crumbed and fried in oil.

1 kg chicken portions
4 chicken drumsticks
7.5 ml (1½ tsp) salt
5 ml (1 tsp) ground cinnamon
4 pieces stick cinnamon
375 ml (1½ cups) dry breadcrumbs
5 ml (1 tsp) cayenne pepper
60 ml (¼ cup) oil
15 ml (1 tbsp) peri-peri oil
1 cardamom pod, split open
3 large eggs, lightly beaten

Wash the chicken pieces, drain and rub with salt and ground cinnamon. Steam in a saucepan in a little water with the stick cinnamon for about 20 minutes. Remove the chicken, drain and set aside to cool. Mix crumbs with cayenne pepper in a bowl. Heat the oils and cardamom in a frying pan. Working quickly, dip the chicken first in the egg, then in the crumbs. Fry the chicken over low heat until crisp and golden brown. Serve with Masala Chips (page 83) and salads.

Serves 6

NOTES:
- An upside-down colander on top of the pan helps the chicken to crisp.
- Another way of coating the chicken with crumbs is to put the breadcrumbs into a plastic or brown paper bag, then drop the chicken into the bag and shake it to ensure a good, even coating.

Malayan Crumbed Chicken

LABARANG OVEN-ROAST CHICKEN

We usually serve this meal at Labarang, the Festival of Charity.

1 x 2 kg fresh chicken
10 ml (2 tsp) salt
2.5 ml (½ tsp) black or white pepper
½ green or red pepper, sliced
1 kg medium potatoes, peeled and sliced or wedged
10 ml (2 tsp) peri-peri oil
10 ml (2 tsp) margarine, melted
125 ml (½ cup) water
5 ml (1 tsp) ground cinnamon

Season the chicken with a little salt and pepper and allow to stand for about 5 minutes. Rub well with a few pepper slices. Put the remaining slices into the chicken cavity. Season the potatoes with salt and pepper. Arrange the chicken and potatoes in a roasting pan and pour over the oil and melted margarine. Add cold water to soften the potatoes and cover with foil. Roast in the oven at 180 °C for about 40 minutes. Remove the foil, reduce the temperature to 160 °C and cook until done. Sprinkle with the cinnamon 5 minutes before serving.
Serves 8

LABARANG GRILLED CHICKENS

First bake the chicken, then grill to crisp the skin.

3 young chickens
1 green pepper, sliced
15 ml (3 tsp) salt
10 ml (2 tsp) red masala
250 g (1 cup) butter or margarine
3 pieces stick cinnamon

Wash and drain the chickens. Rub the skins with some of the green pepper and fill the cavities with the remaining slices. Season with the salt and red masala, and set aside for 30 minutes. Heat the butter or margarine in a heavy-based roasting pan. Add the chickens and cinnamon, and bake, covered, for 30 minutes. Remove the cover and place under the grill. Baste and grill until tender and golden brown, adding a little water to the pan if necessary. Serve with deep-fried sweet potatoes, noodle salad and Malayan Cauliflower (page 82).
Serves 12

DEVILLED CHICKEN

12 chicken drumsticks
½ red or green pepper, sliced
7.5 ml (1½ tsp) salt
5 ml (1 tsp) cayenne pepper
7.5 ml (1½ tsp) red leaf masala
75 g (5 tbsp) butter or margarine
2 pieces stick cinnamon
250 ml (1 cup) water

Wash the drumsticks well. Combine the pepper slices, salt, cayenne pepper and masala, sprinkle over the chicken, and allow to marinate for about 10 minutes. Heat a heavy-based roasting pan over medium heat for 5 minutes. Reduce the heat to low and add the butter. As soon as the butter heats up, add the drumsticks and cinnamon. Grill in a roasting pan, uncovered, for about 15 minutes, then add the water. Cover and cook until the water has been absorbed. Grill again, uncovered, until done (about 45 minutes). Serve with corn and chips.
Serves 6

SWEET AND SOUR CHICKEN

The mixture of tamarind and sugar gives this dish its distinctive sweet-sour flavour.

1 medium-sized chicken, jointed
4 chicken drumsticks
a pinch turmeric
7.5 ml (1½ tsp) tandoori masala
3 cloves garlic, crushed
10 ml (2 tsp) salt
30 ml (2 tbsp) oil
1 large onion, sliced
60 ml (¼ cup) boiling water
10 ml (2 tsp) sugar
60 g (¼ cup) tamarind
10 curry leaves
125 ml (½ cup) water

Wash and drain the chicken. Mix the turmeric, masala, garlic and salt together, rub into the chicken, set aside and marinate for about 10 minutes. Heat the oil in a shallow, heavy-based pan. Toss in the onion and fry until golden brown. Add the chicken and cover the pan for 5 minutes. Meanwhile, add the boiling water and sugar to the tamarind. Allow the chicken to draw, then remove the lid and stir. Add the tamarind and sugar mixture to the chicken by pouring it through a sieve – scrape the sieve with a spoon to let the pulp pass through. Add the curry leaves and cold water to the chicken. Reduce the heat, cover and simmer for about 25 minutes until tender, making sure that the onion does not disintegrate. Serve with Sweet Sultana Yellow Rice (page 81) and Lemon and Kumquat Atjar (page 98).

Serves 6

Sweet and Sour Chicken and Sweet Sultana Yellow Rice (page 81)

SESAME SEED CHICKEN

An interesting flavour combination with the peri-peri oil and sesame seeds.

1 kg chicken portions
6 drumsticks
15 ml (1 tbsp) salt
10 ml (2 tsp) red masala
10 ml (2 tsp) prepared or
home-made chutney
10 ml (2 tsp) tomato sauce
15 ml (1 tbsp) brown vinegar
15 ml (1 tbsp) peri-peri oil
125 g (½ cup) soft margarine
60 ml (¼ cup) sesame seeds

Wash and drain the chicken. Mix the remaining ingredients together, except the sesame seeds, and marinate the chicken for 2 hours. Bake in a large roasting pan at 200 °C for about 40 minutes. Add small amounts of water during cooking to prevent burning. Sprinkle over the sesame seeds 15 minutes before the end of the cooking time. Serve with a favourite noodle salad or salads of your choice.
Serves 6

CHICKEN IN A JIFFY

An easy, flavoursome way to prepare chicken.

1 x 1 kg chicken braai pack
½ green pepper, seeds removed
10 ml (2 tsp) salt
10 ml (2 tsp) red masala
2.5 ml (½ tsp) garum masala
5 ml (1 tsp) fine black pepper
4 whole cloves
30 ml (2 tbsp) soft margarine
10 ml (2 tsp) flour
2 large Jiffy™ cooking bags

Wash and drain the chicken portions, then rub each portion with the inside of the green pepper. Marinate with the salt, spices and margarine, and allow to stand for 30 minutes. Place 5 ml (1 tsp) flour in each Jiffy™ cooking bag and shake. Divide the marinated chicken into two and place in the bags. Secure the bags with the ties provided and pierce them twice on one side with a fork. Bake at 180 °C on the middle shelf of the oven for 45 minutes. Serve with vegetables and deep-fried baby potatoes.
Serves 4

Sesame Seed Chicken

POULTRY STUFFING

30 ml (2 tbsp) white breadcrumbs
500 g sausage meat
(beef sausages without casings)
1 onion, chopped
2.5 ml (½ tsp) dried thyme
2.5 ml (½ tsp) dried tarragon
2.5 ml (½ tsp) fine black pepper
leaf of celery stalk
a pinch ground nutmeg
5 ml (1 tsp) salt
3 dried peaches or apple slices,
roughly chopped
1 egg, beaten with 60 ml (4 tbsp) milk

Combine all the ingredients to form a fairly stiff mixture. Make sure that the stuffing is tightly packed into the chicken or turkey cavity.
Stuffs 1 large chicken or small turkey

GRILLED CAPONS

A special dish to delight your family.

3 capons or baby chickens, halved
500 g medium potatoes, peeled
and halved
½ green pepper, sliced
10 ml (2 tsp) salt
10 ml (2 tsp) leaf masala
250 g (1 cup) margarine
6 pieces stick cinnamon

Wash and drain the capons. Marinate the capons and potatoes with the pepper slices, salt and masala for about 10 minutes. Heat the margarine and cinnamon in a heavy-based roasting pan or saucepan, then add the capons and potatoes a few at a time. Grill at 180 °C for about 35 minutes, turning occasionally, until tender. Remove and keep warm until all the capons and potatoes are cooked. Serve with buttered noodles, corn on the cob and avocado wedges.
Serves 6

MUSCOVY DUCK POT ROAST

A Muscovy duck had greenish-black plumes with white markings and a red caruncle on the bill. It's a messy duck, but tastes so nice!

1 fresh, young Muscovy duck
¼ red or green pepper
10 ml (2 tsp) salt
10 ml (2 tsp) ground black pepper
5 ml (1 tsp) red masala
1 kg small potatoes, peeled
375 ml (1½ cups) oil for
deep-frying
125 g (½ cup) margarine
2 sticks cinnamon

The duck must be well-plucked and washed under slow-running, cold water. Soak the duck in very mildly salted water for 30 minutes. Drain, then marinate by rubbing with red or green pepper first, then the salt, black pepper and masala. Set aside. Meanwhile, deep-fry the potatoes in hot oil and set aside. Strain the potato oil and store for later use. Heat the margarine in a saucepan, add the duck with cinnamon sticks on top and grill, uncovered, over medium heat, adding small amounts of water. Reduce the heat after 40 minutes and add the potatoes to the pan. Serve with a selection of vegetables or salads.
Serves 6

NOTES:
- To remove burns and stains from pots and pans, cook together 375 ml (1½ cups) boiling water, 5 ml (1 tsp) cream of tartar and a squeeze of lemon juice for 15 minutes, then clean pots with a sponge.
- If desired, use the Poultry Stuffing recipe on page 36 to stuff the turkey in the Labarang Turkey recipe below.

LABARANG TURKEY

A special dish for Eid or Christmas.

1 x 2 kg turkey
1 small green pepper, sliced
15 ml (1 tbsp) salt
10 ml (2 tsp) leaf masala
375 ml (1½ cups) water
250 g (1 cup) butter or
margarine, melted
5 ml (1 tsp) finely ground cinnamon
3 cinnamon sticks
2.5 ml (½ tsp) dried thyme
2.5 ml (½ tsp) dried tarragon
2.5 ml (½ tsp) dried oregano
500 g each sweet potatoes and
potatoes, peeled and thickly wedged
a pinch each fine salt and masala
oil for deep-frying

Rub the turkey well with the green pepper, salt and masala. Place in a heavy-based saucepan with the water and steam for about 1 hour. Preheat the oven to 180 °C. Transfer the turkey to a roasting pan and pour the melted butter or margarine over and inside the turkey, then sprinkle with the ground cinnamon. Put the cinnamon sticks on the top of the turkey to enhance the flavour. Roast, uncovered, basting occasionally. Mix the thyme, tarragon and oregano together, and sprinkle over the turkey just before serving. Sprinkle the sweet potatoes and potatoes with the salt and masala, and deep-fry. Serve with salads or noodles with canned fruit salad.
Serves 8

CHAPTER 4

MEAT

Meat, usually served with rice, forms the staple diet of the Malay community. The meat, often braised first, is cooked in a variety of ways. Offal is particularly favoured and is considered a delicacy.

POTROAST LEG OF LAMB

My favourite Eid meal.

1 x 2 kg leg of lamb
10 ml (2 tsp) peri-peri oil
4 cloves garlic, crushed
10 ml (2 tsp) salt
7.5 ml (1½ tsp) pepper
5 ml (1 tsp) red masala
500 ml (2 cups) water
1 small carrot, peeled and sliced
1 kg new potatoes
375 ml (1½ cups) oil

When purchasing the lamb, ask your butcher to remove the gland; alternatively, slit the inside of the leg and remove the gland and cord, which is covered by fat. Make a few incisions in the meat before soaking in lukewarm water for 20 minutes. Rub with the peri-peri oil, garlic, salt, pepper and masala, and place in a roasting saucepan with the water. Cook, covered, for 60 minutes on high, then reduce to medium. Add the carrot to the stock. Baste the meat occasionally for 40 minutes or until tender. Add more water during cooking to make a thick gravy. Deep-fry the potatoes in hot oil and serve with Spicy Carrots and Gem Squash (page 78).
Serves 6–8

Potroast Leg of Lamb

LEFTOVER FARM SPECIAL

Don't throw out any not-so-fresh vegetables – use them in this tasty meal.

60 ml (4 tbsp) oil
1 kg stewing beef
2 onions, chopped
500 ml (2 cups) water
salt to taste
10 ml (2 tsp) leaf masala
1 ripe tomato, grated
½ green chilli, chopped
5 carrots, peeled and cut into pieces
250 g green beans, cut into stubs
1 x 225 g tin green peas

1 small spitskop cabbage (curly top),
   cut into small pieces
500 g potatoes, peeled
   and wedged

Heat the oil in a saucepan and braise the meat and onions until medium brown. Add the water, salt, masala, tomato and chilli, and simmer until the water has cooked away. Now braise a little with small amounts of water. Add the vegetables, except the potatoes, and cook for a further 10 minutes. Add the potatoes and cook until done. Serve with Braised Brown Rice (page 81).

Serves 6

CURRIED MEATBALLS

A fine meal to serve for a Sunday lunch.

SAUCE
60 ml (¼ cup) oil
2 onions, chopped
1 piece stick cinnamon
500 ml (2 cups) water
10 ml (2 tsp) tomato sauce
5 ml (1 tsp) masala
7.5 ml (1½ tsp) turmeric
5 ml (1 tsp) ginger paste
5 ml (1 tsp) salt
1 starseed petal (star anise)
15 ml (1 tbsp) brown vinegar
2 bay leaves
5 ml (1 tsp) sugar
3 allspice
10 ml (2 tsp) dried breadcrumbs

MEATBALLS
4 slices stale bread, soaked in water
for 5 minutes and squeezed dry
15 ml (1 tbsp) chopped parsley
nut of butter
1 tomato, cubed
500 g coarse steak mince

To make the sauce, heat the oil over medium heat and stir-fry three-quarters of the onions. Add the cinnamon and water, then add the tomato sauce, masala, 5 ml (1 tsp) turmeric, ginger paste, 2.5 ml (½ tsp) salt, starseed petal and vinegar. Mix well and leave to simmer. Prepare the meatballs by placing the bread in a basin and adding 2.5 ml (½ tsp) turmeric, parsley, butter, tomato, remaining 2.5 ml (½ tsp) salt and mince. Mix well but lightly and form into medium-sized balls. The sauce should be simmering when the meatballs are added to the saucepan. If necessary, add extra water before adding the meatballs. Reduce the heat and add the bay leaves, sugar, allspice and breadcrumbs. It is important that you do not stir at this stage. Simmer, covered, until done (about 15 minutes). Enjoy with rice and Carrot and Chilli Sambal (page 95).

Serves 4

CABBAGE MEATBALL WRAP

We call this 'koolfrikkadel' – make enough gravy to half-cover the parcels.

60 ml (¼ cup) oil
3 marrow bones
1 onion, chopped
2.5 ml (½ tsp) salt
625 ml (2½ cups) water
1 medium spitskop cabbage (curly top)
5 ml (1 tsp) ground black pepper
5 ml (1 tsp) ground nutmeg
4 whole cloves
6 allspice
2 bay leaves
60 g (¼ cup) butter
10 ml (2 tsp) fine, dry breadcrumbs

MEATBALLS
5 slices stale bread, soaked in water
for 5 minutes and squeezed dry
1 kg steak mince
7.5 ml (1½ tsp) salt
1 egg
10 ml (2 tsp) chopped parsley

Heat the oil in a large, shallow saucepan and add the marrow bones, onion, salt and 250 ml (1 cup) water. Braise until golden-brown. Separate the cabbage into leaves, removing the veins but leaving a bit of stalk, and wash well. Add the remaining 375 ml (1½ cups) water to the saucepan. Place the cabbage leaves on top of the meat and steam for about 10 minutes, covered, until the leaves are half-cooked and brown. Remove from the stove. To make the meatballs, place the bread in a mixing bowl, add the mince and remaining meatball ingredients plus 2.5 ml (½ tsp) each of pepper and nutmeg. Mix well, using a spoon. The texture must be fairly loose. Using your hands, shape the mince mixture into balls about the size of golf balls. Remove the cabbage leaves from the saucepan with a slotted spoon. Place a meatball in the centre of each cabbage leaf, roll up into parcels and set aside on a platter. Return the saucepan to the stove and bring to the boil over medium heat. The moment the gravy begins to cook, return the cabbage parcels to the pan and sprinkle over the remaining pepper and nutmeg, cloves, allspice, bay leaves and butter, cut into small pieces. Finally, add the breadcrumbs, cover, and steam on low heat for about 20 minutes. Serve the cabbage parcels on a bed of white rice.
Serves 6

NOTE: To tenderise meat for frying, pour 10 ml (2 tsp) vinegar over the meat, rub it in and leave for 10 minutes. Then pound the meat with the bottom of a heavy stoneware mug or saucer (it's an old wive's tale, but it works!). Do this a few times, then cook as desired.

Cabbage Meatball Wrap served with Long-grain White Rice (page 81)

BRAISED STEAK MINCE

I often use this as a filling for rotis (page 142).

60 ml (¼ cup) oil
1 large onion, chopped
1 small tomato, blanched, peeled
and pulped
1 kg coarse steak mince
1 green pepper, chopped
2.5 ml (½ tsp) red masala
1 small green chilli, chopped
2.5 ml (½ tsp) crushed garlic
10 ml (2 tsp) salt
1 whole clove
4 allspice
500 g small potatoes, peeled
and quartered
60 ml (¼ cup) water

Using a heavy-based saucepan, heat the oil over medium heat and toss in the onion. Stir-fry until well browned. Add the remaining ingredients. Stir thoroughly and cook, covered, for 5 minutes, then reduce the heat and simmer until the potatoes are soft.

Serves 5 as a main meal

LAMBS' HEARTS AND SOURS

For those who like offal, this is a dish you'll really enjoy.

4 lambs' hearts, washed and sliced
into thin rings
2.5 ml (½ tsp) salt
2.5 ml (½ tsp) leaf masala
250 ml (1 cup) water
60 ml (¼ cup) oil
1 medium onion, sliced
4 slices red or green pepper
15 ml (1 tbsp) brown vinegar
5 ml (1 tsp) sugar

Sprinkle salt and masala over the heart slices. Over a medium heat, cook the meat in water for 20 minutes. Now add most of the oil and continue to cook until the meat starts to fry. Stir continuously and rapidly until light brown, then remove from the heat. Cover and set aside in a preheated warming drawer. Using a separate pan, heat the remaining oil and toss in the onion. Braise a little, then add the sliced pepper, vinegar, sugar and a pinch of salt. Turn off the heat. Spoon this mixture over the hearts. This is a delicious meal with warm corn on the cob, buttered Brussels sprouts and Light Brown Rolls (page 138).

Serves 3

MALAYAN BOBOTIE

60 ml (¼ cup) oil
1 medium onion, chopped
4 cloves garlic, slivered
2.5 ml (½ tsp) curry powder
2 bay leaves, torn
5 ml (1 tsp) red masala
10 ml (2 tsp) salt
6 slices stale bread, soaked in water for 5 minutes and squeezed dry
30 ml (2 tbsp) butter or margarine
1 kg steak mince
4 eggs

Heat 15 ml oil (1 tbsp) in a saucepan over medium heat. Add the onion, garlic, curry powder, bay leaves, masala and salt. Reduce the heat to low and braise the onion lightly. Add the bread, stir a couple of times and cook for 5 minutes. Remove from the heat and allow to cool. Stir in the butter and mince, and transfer to an ovenproof glass dish. Bake at 180 °C for 30 minutes. Beat the eggs well, adding 15 ml (1 tbsp) cold water. Remove the bobotie from the oven and pour the egg over the top. Return to the oven and bake, uncovered, for 5–10 minutes. Serve with yellow rice and salads.

Serves 8

SPECIAL LASAGNE

The pasta is homemade, there's no white sauce and the meat is deliciously spiced.

60 ml (¼ cup) oil
1 large onion, chopped
5 cloves garlic, crushed
1 kg coarse steak mince
1 starseed petal (star anise)
½ red or green pepper, cut into strips
1 x 65 g tin tomato paste
10 ml (2 tsp) medium-coarse salt
7.5 ml (1½ tsp) tandoori masala
2.5 ml (½ tsp) turmeric
10 ml (2 tsp) white sugar
1 small green chilli, chopped
250 ml (1 cup) fresh orange juice
200 g Parmesan or Cheddar cheese, coarsely grated
5 ml (1 tsp) dried oregano
5 ml (1 tsp) dried thyme

PASTA
2 eggs
2 cups flour
2.5 ml (½ tsp) salt
2.5 ml (½ tsp) masala
2.5 ml (½ tsp) dried tarragon

2.5 ml (½ tsp) dried thyme
2.5 ml (½ tsp) dried oregano
375 ml (1½ cups) lukewarm water

First make the meat sauce. Heat the oil in a large saucepan on medium-high. Add the onion and garlic, and sauté until transparent. Now add the mince and cook until well browned. Add the rest of the ingredients, except the orange juice, cheese, oregano and thyme, and cook for a few minutes, stirring occasionally. Reduce the heat to low, add the orange juice and simmer for about 10 minutes or until the sauce is fairly thick but not dry. Remove from the heat and leave to cool. To make the pasta, mix all the ingredients together to form a soft, pliable dough. If the dough is too crumbly, add a few drops of water. If it's too wet and sticks to the bowl, add a little extra flour. Roll out on a floured surface as thinly as possible and cut into strips, about 5 x 20 cm. Boil the water in a deep saucepan. Drop the strips of dough into the boiling water, reduce the heat and cook for 5–7 minutes. Remove with a slotted spoon and set aside. Continue in this way until all the dough has been cooked. Line a well-greased ovenproof dish with the pasta strips and fill with the meat mixture. Alternatively, layer the meat and pasta, ending with a layer of pasta. Sprinkle over the grated cheese, thyme and oregano and heat through on the middle shelf of the oven at 180 °C for about 15 minutes or until the cheese has melted. Serve hot with Beetroot and Onion Salad (page 85) and Cucumber Salad (page 86).

Serves 6

HAZENDAL PUMPKIN

One winter afternoon, I saw four Hazendal women returning from the abattoir with offal (which was then given away free) and dividing it amongst themselves – I devised this recipe with them in mind.

2 kg sheep or ox tripe, cleaned
60 ml (¼ cup) oil
2 marrow bones
I onion, chopped
I kg pumpkin or hubbard squash, sliced or cubed
2.5 ml (½ tsp) turmeric
7.5 ml (1½ tsp) salt
I starseed petal (star anise)
I chilli or a pinch cayenne pepper
4 slices red or green pepper
7.5 ml (1½ tsp) fresh ginger
10 ml (2 tsp) sugar

It is important that tripe be well cooked. Sheep tripe takes 2 hours and ox tripe 3 hours to cook in a saucepan, and both will take about 1 hour in a pressure cooker. Cut the tripe into strips about 6 x 2 cm and set aside. Heat the oil in a broad saucepan over medium heat, add the bones and onion, and braise until well-browned. Now add the pumpkin, turmeric, salt, starseed and chilli. Cook, uncovered, for about 30 minutes, stirring once or twice. When the pumpkin starts drying out, reduce the heat and add the sliced pepper, ginger, sugar and tripe. Simmer for about 10 minutes – do not add any water unless absolutely necessary. Serve with rice and chutney.

Serves 4–5

KOUE BOKKEVELD SPECIAL

500 g (2½ cups) dried peas, soaked overnight
60 ml (¼ cup) oil
I onion, sliced
I ox trotter, precooked
½ green pepper, chopped
½ green chilli
I starseed petal (star anise)
7.5 ml (1½ sp) salt
10 ml (2 tsp) sugar

Rinse the dried peas well and cook until soft. Remove any shells that rise to the surface, and drain. Heat the oil in a saucepan over medium heat. Braise the onion until golden brown. Now add the trotter, peas and remaining ingredients to the saucepan and simmer over a very low heat for 10 minutes. Enjoy with chutney and rice.

Serves 6

LIVER AND ONION

An all-time favourite Malay supper.

1 kg sheep liver, film removed and cut into thin slices
5 ml (1 tsp) salt
5 ml (1 tsp) ground black pepper
60 ml (¼ cup) vinegar or
60 ml (¼ cup) milk
250 ml (1 cup) oil
125 ml (½ cup) cake flour
a pinch ground or grated nutmeg
4 small onions, sliced
1 red or green chilli, halved

Wash and dry the liver. Season with salt and pepper, add the vinegar or milk, and set aside for 1 hour. Heat the oil in a skillet over medium heat until medium hot. Remove the liver from the milk or vinegar, and allow excess liquid to drip off. Dip into the flour mixed with the nutmeg and fry. Using a fork, turn the liver quickly until done. If it is cooked for too long, it will become tough. Braise the onions with the chilli in a small pan until golden brown, then flavour with a little vinegar and sugar. Serve immediately with mashed potatoes and steamed gem squash.

Serves 6

LABARANG CORNED BEEF

My Labarang speciality.

2 kg topside beef
2 litres (8 cups) water
1 bay leaf
1 whole clove
15 ml (1 tbsp) coriander seeds
60 g (¼ cup) saltpetre (obtainable from a pharmacy)
250 g (1 cup) coarse salt

Using a knife with a sharp point, make about 10 slits in the meat, 2.5 cm deep and wide enough to press spices into them. Boil the water and add the bay leaf, clove and 5 ml (1 tsp) coriander, slightly crushed. Wet the meat with the hands, but do not wash. Working in a broad enamel or porcelain mixing bowl, fill the holes in the meat first with saltpetre and salt. Be careful that you do not have any open cuts on your hands. Allow the meat to stand for 5 minutes, then wet the meat again and allow it to stand for a further 5 minutes. Lastly insert three-quarters of the coriander seeds and sprinkle the remainder on top. Saltpetre melts the moment it makes contact with the wet meat but salt takes a little longer. Leave the meat to stand in a very cool place overnight and turn every 6 hours. On the following day, pour in 500 ml (2 cups) cold water. Leave to stand for 2 more days, turning occasionally. On the third day, rinse lightly and cook in 1.5 litres (6 cups) water until soft. Dilute the water if too salty. If using a pressure cooker, cook for about 1 hour. If using a saucepan, it will take about 2½ hours. Use the same water in which to boil your vegetables or steam them.

Serves 6–8

Liver and Onion

CHAPTER 5

CURRIES AND BREYANIS

*Malay curry is sweeter than an Indian one and is usually
served with rice or rotis and sambals. Also very popular,
a breyani is a semi-dry dish of rice, spices and meat,
chicken or fish, served in one pot.*

MINCED PERLEMOEN CURRY

Vary this dish by adding fried brinjal wedges or early garden peas.

30 ml (2 tbsp) oil
1 medium onion, chopped
1 small tomato, blanched, peeled and pulped
2 small pieces stick cinnamon
4 allspice
2 whole cloves
2 cardamom pods, split open
2.5 ml (½ tsp) garlic and ginger paste
2.5 ml (½ tsp) red masala
a pinch turmeric
a pinch ground jeera (cumin)
5 curry leaves
2.5 ml (½ tsp) medium-coarse salt
2 perlemoen, well cleaned and minced

Heat the oil in a skillet and add the onion. Braise until well browned. Add the tomato, then the remaining ingredients, including the perlemoen. Simmer for 25 minutes over low heat. Perlemoen has natural juices, so do not add water unless absolutely necessary. Serve hot on a bed of rice.
Serves 5

HOUT BAY CRAYFISH TAIL CURRY

Make sure that the shell and the tail of the crayfish are slit open and the alimentary canal extracted before cooking.

1 x 3 cm block tamarind
125 ml (½ cup) boiling water
10 ml (2 tsp) sugar
60 ml (¼ cup) oil
1 large onion, chopped
45 ml (3 tbsp) tomato purée
5 ml (1 tsp) turmeric
5 ml (1 tsp) red masala
625 ml (2½ cups) water
3 medium, fresh or frozen crayfish tails, quartered
1 small tomato, blanched, peeled and pulped
5 ml (1 tsp) garlic and ginger paste
1 starseed petal (star anise)
10 curry leaves
5 whole cloves
5 allspice
4 pieces stick cinnamon
4 cardamom pods, split open
5 ml (1 tsp) salt
5 ml (1 tsp) ground jeera (cumin)

Soak the tamarind in the boiling water and sugar for about 2 minutes. Strain and set the liquid aside. Heat the oil in a broad, heavy-based saucepan over medium heat. Add the onion and braise until golden brown. Add the tomato purée, turmeric, masala and 125 ml (½ cup) water; reduce the heat to low. Add the crayfish tails, tomato pulp and remaining ingredients, except the jeera and tamarind liquid, to the saucepan and cook slowly. Add the remaining 500 ml (2 cups) water, jeera and tamarind liquid. Add more sugar to taste, cover and simmer gently. Do not remove the lid until ready to serve with fluffy white rice and lemon wedges.
Serves 5

NOTE: Soft fish in a curry will shred easily.

Hout Bay Crayfish Tail Curry

SNOEK CURRY

The dhania (coriander) leaves enhance the flavour of the snoek.

60 ml (¼ cup) oil
half a small snoek, cut into steaks
10 ml (2 tsp) salt
7.5 ml (1½ tsp) red roasted masala
flour for dusting
4 pieces stick cinnamon
1 large onion, chopped
10 ml (2 tsp) tomato sauce
1 small tomato, blanched, peeled
and pulped
4 slices green pepper
5 ml (1 tsp) crushed garlic
5 ml (1 tsp) turmeric
4 whole cloves
8 allspice
1 starseed petal (star anise)
2 cardamom pods, split open
60 g (¼ cup) tamarind, soaked in
125 ml (½ cup) boiling water with
10 ml (2 tsp) sugar

60 g (¼ cup) green dhania
(coriander) leaves, torn, or
10 curry leaves

Heat 30 ml (2 tbsp) oil in a heavy-based saucepan over medium heat. Lightly dust the fish with salt, 2.5 ml (½ tsp) masala and a little flour. Fry lightly, adding more oil if necessary. Remove the fish from the pan and drain. Now heat the cinnamon and onion in the remaining oil. Add the tomato sauce and pulp. Reduce the heat and add the remaining ingredients, except the tamarind and dhania, stirring a few times and adding a small amount of water. Allow to simmer. Scoop out some of the sauce and mix with the strained tamarind liquid. Arrange the fish in a saucepan and cover with the sauce and tamarind. Before serving, add the dhania leaves. Serve hot with Braised Brown Rice (page 81).
Serves 6

BLACK-EYED BEAN CURRY

It's well worth making this tasty, nutritious meal, despite the somewhat lengthy procedure.

500 g (2½ cups) black-eyed beans,
soaked overnight in boiling water
and drained
60 ml (¼ cup) oil
3 pieces stick cinnamon
1 large onion, chopped
500 g shoulder of mutton, cubed
500 g mutton thick rib or knuckle
15 ml (1 tbsp) tomato sauce or purée
5 ml (1 tsp) turmeric
5 ml (1 tsp) red masala
375 ml (1½ cups) water
10 curry leaves
5 ml (1 tsp) sugar
5 ml (1 tsp) garlic and
ginger paste
5 ml (1 tsp) salt
2.5 ml (½ tsp) ground jeera (cumin)
1 starseed petal (star anise)

Cook the beans in salted water until soft and set aside. Heat the oil in a heavy-based saucepan over medium heat and scorch the cinnamon and onion until golden brown. Now add the meat, tomato sauce or purée, turmeric, masala and 250 ml (1 cup) water. Cook until the liquid has been absorbed. Stir well and add the remaining 125 ml (½ cup) water. Simmer until the meat is tender. Add the beans and remaining ingredients, stir thoroughly, reduce the heat and simmer covered.
Serves 6

TAMARIND FISH CURRY

Red roman or red or white stumpnose can be used instead of Cape salmon.

1 kg Cape salmon, thickly sliced
10 ml (2 tsp) salt
125 ml (½ cup) oil
5 cardamom pods, split open
4 pieces stick cinnamon
1 large onion, chopped
5 ml (1 tsp) turmeric
10 ml (2 tsp) leaf masala
500 ml (2 cups) water
20 ml (1½ tbsp) tomato purée
60 g (¼ cup) tamarind,
soaked in 125 ml (¼ cup)
boiling water with
10 ml (2 tsp) sugar
20 curry leaves
2 starseed petals (star anise)
4 whole cloves
8 allspice
2 bay leaves

Wash and dry the fish. Season with the salt. Heat the oil in a pan over medium heat and fry the fish with 2 cardamom pods until semi-cooked. Remove from the heat and allow to cool. Drain the oil from the fish for further use. Using a broad saucepan and the same oil, add the remaining 3 cardamom pods and cinnamon; heat well. Braise the onion, then add the turmeric, masala, water and tomato purée. Bring slowly to the boil and gently add the fried fish. Pour the strained tamarind liquid over the fish. Add the remaining ingredients and stir well, but gently, so as not to break up the fish. Allow to simmer over a low heat. Add more water if the sauce is too dry. A delicious way to serve this dish is with white rice, Braised Tomato (page 78) and Lemon and Brinjal Atjar (page 97).

Serves 6

PENANG CURRY

A fairly dry but flavoursome curry that originates from the island of Penang in Java.

1.5 kg lamb cutlet chops, tenderised
with a light mallet
5 ml (1 tsp) turmeric
5 ml (1 tsp) red masala
5 ml (1 tsp) crushed garlic
10 ml (2 tsp) salt
60 ml (¼ cup) oil
2 cardamom pods, crushed
4 small pieces stick cinnamon
1 large onion, sliced lengthwise
250 ml (1 cup) water
15 ml (1 tbsp) brown vinegar
7.5 ml (1½ tsp) sugar
1 starseed petal (star anise)
2 bay leaves
4 whole cloves
6 allspice
10 ml (2 tsp) dry breadcrumbs

Wash and drain the chops well in a colander and allow to stand for 5 minutes. Marinate the chops with the turmeric, masala and garlic for 1 hour. Add 7.5 ml (1½ tsp) salt. Heat the oil in a frying pan and add the crushed cardamom. Add the chops and fry lightly for 5 minutes on each side. Remove and place in another dish. In a broad, heavy-based saucepan, add the cinnamon and oil from the frying pan, and fry the onion lightly. Add the meat (the onion should partly cover the meat) and cook for 30 minutes in 125 ml (½ cup) water, making sure that the onion is not cooked away. Do not stir. Add the rest of the water, cover, reduce the heat and simmer – this is a semi-dry curry. Pour the vinegar into a cup, add the sugar and stir well. Pour over the meat with the remaining salt, starseed petal and other spices. Stir in the breadcrumbs. Enjoy with yellow rice and salads.

Serves 6

Vegetable Curry (opposite) served with Long-Grain White Rice (page 81)

CHICKEN CURRY

A meal in itself! Serve with rotis and a favourite sambal.

1 kg chicken portions
7.5 ml (1½ tsp) finely chopped fresh ginger
4 cloves garlic, finely chopped
30 ml (2 tbsp) oil
6 cardamom pods
6 pieces stick cinnamon
1 large onion, finely chopped
30 ml (2 tbsp) tomato purée
5 ml (1 tsp) turmeric
5 ml (1 tsp) leaf masala
250 ml (1 cup) water
10 ml (2 tsp) salt
10 curry leaves
1 starseed petal (star anise)
500 g potatoes, peeled and quartered
375 ml (1½ cups) water
5 ml (1 tsp) barishap (fennel seeds)
5 ml (1 tsp) ground jeera (cumin)

Wash and drain the chicken well. Marinate with the ginger and garlic for a few minutes. Heat the oil in a saucepan and add the cardamom and cinnamon. Add the onion and stir until golden brown. Now add the tomato purée, turmeric, leaf masala and water. Add the chicken, salt, curry leaves and starseed to the saucepan with the potatoes, and cook for 15 minutes. Add the remaining ingredients, reduce the heat and stir well but gently to blend the ingredients. Allow to simmer for about 30 minutes until the chicken is tender. Add more water if necessary. Serve with rice or Malay Roti (page 142).

Serves 6

NOTE: When using cup measurements, use a standard kitchen cup.

VEGETABLE CURRY

A delicious vegetarian curry that can be made with any vegetables in season. As a variation, small, hard-boiled eggs can also be added.

½ small spitskop cabbage (curly top), stalks removed and finely shredded
2 baby gem squashes, cut into quarters, pips removed
½ bunch baby carrots, peeled and sliced
3 medium potatoes, peeled and quartered
60 ml (¼ cup) oil
1 piece stick cinnamon
2 cardamom pods, split open
1 small onion, chopped
15 ml (1 tbsp) tomato sauce
1 small tomato, blanched, peeled and pulped
5 ml (1 tsp) leaf masala
5 ml (1 tsp) turmeric
1 starseed petal (star anise)

5 ml (1 tsp) salt
250 ml (1 cup) water
2.5 ml (½ tsp) sugar
2.5 ml (½ tsp) ground jeera (cumin)
8 curry leaves

Soak the vegetables in cold water until clean, then drain in a colander. Heat the oil in a saucepan and braise the cinnamon, cardamom and onion until golden brown. Add the tomato sauce, tomato pulp, masala, turmeric, starseed petal and salt. Braise, then add the water. Add the vegetables to the saucepan, stir gently and mix in the sugar. Cook, covered, for another 15 minutes on medium heat, then sprinkle over the jeera and steam until done, making sure that the dish has a fair amount of gravy. The curry leaves must be added 5 minutes before the dish is ready to serve. Enjoy with Apple Sambal (page 95) and white rice tinted with a pinch of turmeric and flavoured with one piece of stick cinnamon.

Serves 4

LAMB CUTLET AND BRINJAL CURRY

I was honoured to serve this dish to the Japanese consul, his wife and secretary a few years ago – it was a great success!

1.5 kg lean lamb cutlets
2 large onions, chopped
30 ml (2 tbsp) chopped green pepper
15 ml (1 tbsp) medium-coarse salt
10 ml (2 tsp) crushed fresh ginger
10 ml (2 tsp) tandoori masala
a pinch turmeric
15 ml (1 tbsp) tomato sauce
125 ml (½ cup) cold water
2 large brinjals, cut into wedges
5 ml (1 tsp) ground jeera (cumin)
1 starseed petal (star anise)
5 ml (1 tsp) sugar
10 curry leaves with stalks

Cut the rind of fat off the cutlets. Wash well and arrange in a large, shallow, heavy-based saucepan. Top with the onion, green pepper, salt, ginger, masala, turmeric and tomato sauce. Allow to simmer, covered, over medium heat for about 20 minutes. Remove the lid and stir thoroughly. Add the cold water and brinjal wedges. Reduce the heat, cover and simmer for a further 20 minutes. Add the remaining spices, sugar and curry leaves. This is a semi-dry dish, so there should not be too much sauce but just enough to keep it moist. Serve with Cinnamon Rice (page 81) and Apple Sambal (page 95).

Serves 8

MUNG DHAL CURRY

Mung Dhal are tiny green peas, also known as Chinese peas.

1 kg tenderised steak, cubed
2 marrow bones
15 ml (1 tbsp) masala
5 ml (1 tsp) turmeric
5 ml (1 tsp) ginger paste
60 ml (¼ cup) oil
1 onion, chopped
3 cardamom pods, split open
4 pieces stick cinnamon
5 ml (1 tsp) salt
½ green pepper
15 ml (1 tbsp) tomato sauce
5 ml (1 tsp) garlic
2 small green chillies, chopped
10 curry leaves
5 ml (1 tsp) sugar
250 ml (1 cup) water
500 g (2½ cups) mung dhal (Chinese peas), soaked overnight in water, drained and cooked until soft
5 ml (1 tsp) ground jeera (cumin)
1 tomato, blanched, peeled and pulped

Wash the meat and drain. Mix together the masala, turmeric and ginger paste, rub into the steak and allow to marinate for a few minutes. Heat the oil in a heavy-based saucepan over medium heat. Add the onion, cardamom, cinnamon and marrow bones. Braise until golden brown. Add the remaining ingredients, except the water, mung dhal, jeera and tomato, and cook for 30 minutes. Lastly add the water, mung dhal, jeera and tomato. Enjoy this meal with Malay Roti (page 142) or Khitchri Rice (page 80) and a relish of Lemon and Brinjal Atjar (page 97).

Serves 6

Opposite: Lamb Cutlet and Brinjal Curry

CHICKEN BREYANI

Since saffron is so expensive, food colouring is used here as a substitute. This adds colour; saffron, however, adds flavour as well as colour.

1 kg chicken portions
6 small drumsticks
2 onions, sliced
15 ml (1 tbsp) oil
250 g (2½ cups) lentils
500 g (2½ cups) uncooked long-grain white rice
10 ml (2 tsp) margarine
4 pieces stick cinnamon
4 cardamom pods, split open
3 green chillies, chopped
12 small eggs, hard-boiled and peeled
10 ml (2 tsp) jeera (cumin) seeds or gharum masala
2.5 ml (½ tsp) egg yellow food colouring mixed with
125 ml (½ cup) boiling water

MARINADE
250 ml (1 cup) buttermilk or stirred yoghurt
10 ml (2 tsp) red masala
7.5 ml (1½ tsp) turmeric
15 ml (1 tbsp) peri-peri oil
10 ml (2 tsp) garlic and ginger paste
5 ml (1 tsp) ground cinnamon
15 ml (1 tbsp) salt

Wash the chicken. Combine the marinade ingredients and marinate the chicken for 2 hours. Fry the onions in heated oil until golden brown. Set aside. Cook the lentils in rapidly boiling water, drain and set aside. Cook the rice, strain, drain, steam and set aside. Heat the margarine in a heavy-based, large saucepan and toss in the cinnamon and cardamom. Add the chicken and brown over medium heat. Buttermilk and yoghurt burn easily, so add small amounts of cold water as it browns. The water will prevent the chicken from sticking to the pan. Cook, uncovered, for 1 hour and remove from the heat. In a large dish, mix the rice, lentils, onion, chillies and chicken. Transfer half of this mixture to the saucepan and heat through. Make holes with a spoon handle in the breyani and insert the whole eggs. Sprinkle with half of the jeera, then add the remaining breyani and sprinkle with the remaining jeera, egg yellow and water. Keep covered on low heat until ready to serve with Green Bean Smoor (page 85) and Cinnamon Pumpkin (page 78).
Serves 6

PENSLAWER

A popular curry even though the tripe takes some time to prepare.

1.5 kg sheep or ox tripe, cleaned
1 litre (4 cups) water
60 ml (¼ cup) oil
2 pieces stick cinnamon
2 cardamom pods, slightly cracked
1 onion, chopped
5 ml (1 tsp) salt
5 ml (1 tsp) turmeric
1 bay leaf, halved
5 ml (1 tsp) red masala
1 starseed petal (star anise)
5 ml (1 tsp) garlic and ginger paste
15 ml (1 tbsp) tomato purée, pulp of
½ tomato or 10 ml (2 tsp) tomato sauce
8 curry leaves
2.5 ml (½ tsp) ground jeera (cumin)

Cut the tripe into 6 x 2 cm slices. Cook in the water over medium heat. Sheep tripe takes 2 hours and ox tripe 3 hours in a saucepan; both will take about 1 hour to cook in a pressure cooker. Cook the tripe until tender and set aside before using it for the curry. Heat the oil in a heavy-based saucepan. Toss in the cinnamon and cardamom. Add the onion and scorch until golden brown. Add the salt, tripe and remaining ingredients, except the jeera. Simmer for 30 minutes until done. Finally add the jeera and allow to stand for a few minutes before serving with rice and Apple Sambal (page 95).
Serves 5

AKHNI

60 ml (¼ cup) oil
1.5 kg mutton thin ribs
2 onions, chopped
6 small pieces stick cinnamon
4 cardamom pods
500 ml (2 cups) water
500 g (2½ cups) parboiled brown rice
5 ml (1 tsp) turmeric
10 ml (2 tsp) salt
½ green pepper
5 ml (1 tsp) leaf masala
4 whole cloves
10 ml (2 tsp) garlic and ginger paste
1 starseed petal (star anise)
1 red or green chilli, halved
5 ml (1 tsp) gharum masala
20 curry leaves and stalks
20 ml (1½ tbsp) tomato sauce
2 thick slices tomato
5 ml (1 tsp) sugar

Heat the oil in a large saucepan over medium heat. Arrange the meat on the bottom of the saucepan, followed by the onion, 4 pieces stick cinnamon and cardamom pods. Cook without water, uncovered, allowing the meat to draw water. Braise until dry. Add the water and continue to cook, covered, on medium heat. In the meantime, cook the rice in rapidly boiling water with the turmeric, salt and remaining 2 pieces of stick cinnamon. Drain in a colander and steam for 20 minutes. Set aside to cool until later. To save time, the rice can be prepared in advance and kept in the fridge until needed. Add the remaining ingredients, except the rice, to the meat mixture, reduce the heat to low, and stir gently. When the meat is tender and juicy, mix in the rice. When the meat and rice have heated through, remove from the heat. Serve hot with buttered new potatoes, salads and Tomato and Mint Sambal (page 95).
Serves 8

NOTES:
- In the Akhni recipe, the curry and rice are served in one pot, which makes it a practical and popular dish when catering for large functions or ceremonies.
- To give fish and potatoes a good colour, sprinkle a few drops of lemon juice over them before cooking.
- Keep flies out of the kitchen by hanging a tomato plant or a mint sprig from the ceiling. Get rid of ants and cockroaches by sprinkling a mixture of salt and borax along the back of shelves.

PRAWN BREYANI

Leaving the shells on the prawns enhances the flavour of the breyani.

I kg fresh or frozen prawns, deveined
7.5 ml (1½ tsp) tandoori masala
10 ml (2 tsp) salt
750 g (3¾ cups) uncooked
long-grain white rice
I small onion, chopped
375 ml (1½ cups) oil
4 green or red pepper slices
2 pieces stick cinnamon
I starseed petal (star anise)
4 cardamom pods, split open
I large onion, sliced
5 ml (1 tsp) turmeric
15 ml (1 tbsp) tomato sauce
5 ml (1 tsp) garlic and ginger paste
200 ml (¾ cup) cold water
5 whole cloves
5 ml (1 tsp) gharum masala

Wash the prawns and marinate with the masala and salt. Set aside. Cook the rice in rapidly boiling salted water in a broad saucepan. Drain and set aside. Toss the small chopped onion into 10 ml (2 tsp) warm oil and fry lightly until golden brown. Add the pepper slices, a small piece of stick cinnamon and starseed petal. Remove from the pan when just done. Using a heavy-based pan over medium heat, lightly fry the prawns in the remaining oil with one crushed cardamom pod until all the prawns have been fried. Set aside. Using only 30 ml (2 tbsp) of the oil that the prawns were fried in, braise the large chopped onion until golden brown. Add the remaining ingredients, except the cloves and gharum masala. Stir a few times and turn off the heat. Dish out three-quarters of the sauce into the pot, then layer the rice, prawns and another layer of rice in the pot, sprinkling over the cloves and gharum masala. Slow-steam for 12–15 minutes, then remove from the heat and serve with a favourite sambal and Braised Tomato (page 78).

Serves 6

STEAK, KIDNEY AND BRINJAL KEDGEREE

A kedgeree is similar to a breyani in that it's a semi-dry meal with a little gravy.

I small brinjal, sliced
5 ml (1 tsp) salt
a pinch red leaf masala
60 ml (¼ cup) oil
500 g (2½ cups) parboiled white rice
3 whole cloves
500 g tenderised steak, cubed
4 lambs' kidneys, soaked in
10 ml (2 tsp) brown vinegar, drained
and cubed
I onion, sliced in rings
½ green pepper, sliced into rings
2 cloves garlic, crushed
2 potatoes, peeled and cubed
3 small carrots, peeled and boiled
4 pieces stick cinnamon
6 allspice
I x 410 g tin whole-kernel corn,
drained
2 tomatoes, cut into wedges and
sprinkled with a little sugar

Place the brinjal slices in lightly salted water to prevent discoloration. Set aside to drain. Sprinkle with 2.5 ml (½ tsp) of the salt and the masala. Fry in 30 ml (2 tbsp) oil until tender and set aside. Boil the rice with the cloves, then strain, steam and set aside to cool. Heat the remaining 30 ml (2 tbsp) oil in a heavy-based saucepan and add the steak and kidneys. Cook for 30 minutes, adding water if necessary and stirring occasionally. Add the onion, green pepper and garlic, and fry for a further 10 minutes, then add the remaining ingredients, except the tomato wedges, and remove from the heat. Layer the rice, steak and kidney and brinjal in a casserole dish, ending with a layer of meat. If necessary, heat through in the oven before serving with the tomato wedges, Cabbage Smoor (page 83) and Apple Sambal (page 95).

Serves 4–6

Prawn Breyani

CHAPTER 6

BREDIES AND STEWS

A bredie is a type of stew, slowly simmered – the type of vegetable used gives it its name. Stews are favoured as everyday meals, with a variety of ingredients used and always deliciously spiced.

TOMATO BREDIE

A very popular dish with Cape Malays, it is best made with fresh, ripe tomatoes. Tomato paste must be added for flavour if canned tomatoes are used. Use 1 x 410 g tin tomatoes and 5 ml (1 tsp) tomato paste instead of fresh tomatoes.

1 kg stewing beef, cubed
60 ml (¼ cup) oil
1 onion, chopped
3 marrow bones
500 g tomatoes, blanched, peeled and pulped
10 ml (2 tsp) tomato paste
5 ml (1 tsp) salt
15 ml (1 tbsp) sugar
1 green chilli, chopped
¼ green pepper, sliced
1 kg small or medium potatoes, peeled and halved
2.5 ml (½ tsp) turmeric
2.5 ml (½ tsp) leaf masala

Wash and drain the meat. Heat the oil in a large saucepan on medium heat and toss in the beef, onion and bones. Braise until well browned. Now add the tomato, tomato paste, salt, sugar, chilli, pepper slices and potatoes. Stir well. Cook for 20 minutes, then reduce the heat. Add the turmeric and masala; continue to simmer, uncovered, until the meat is tender. Serve with Long-grain White Rice (page 81).
Serves 6

NOTE: A pinch of turmeric added to a tomato stew or bredie gives it a lovely rich colour.

TOMATO-CHICKEN BREDIE

15 ml (1 tbsp) oil
1 medium onion, chopped
1 kg chicken drumsticks
250 g chicken necks, well-washed
500 g ripe tomatoes, blanched, peeled and roughly chopped
½ green chilli, chopped
5 ml (1 tsp) salt
5 ml (1 tsp) tomato paste
a pinch turmeric
10 ml (2 tsp) sugar
1 starseed petal (star anise)
5 ml (1 tsp) dried thyme

Heat the oil in a saucepan over medium heat. Toss in the onion and braise until golden brown. Add the chicken portions and braise for 10 minutes. Add the remaining ingredients, except the thyme, and simmer, uncovered, for about 45 minutes. Lastly add the thyme, remove from the stove and serve hot with Lemon and Kumquat Atjar (page 98) and Cinnamon Rice (page 81).
Serves 6

BABY GREEN PEA BREDIE

This one has an added kick from the chilli.

500 g mutton knuckles
1 medium onion, chopped
10 ml (2 tsp) medium-coarse salt
about 500 ml (2 cups) water
15 ml (1 tbsp) oil
500 g lamb cutlets
1 small starseed petal (star anise)
5 ml (1 tsp) red masala
5 ml (1 tsp) sugar
500 g fresh baby peas, shelled, or frozen peas
1 green chilli, chopped
500 g new potatoes
5 ml (1 tsp) dried thyme

Set a heavy-based saucepan on medium heat. Add the knuckles, onion, salt and 250 ml (1 cup) water, and cook until dry. Then add the oil and braise until lightly browned. Add the cutlets and braise further with a little more water until the food has browned completely. Add remaining ingredients, except the thyme and remaining water, and simmer, uncovered, for 45 minutes or until tender. Add the thyme and the remaining 250 ml (1 cup) water 15 minutes before the end of the cooking time. Reduce the heat and simmer. Serve hot with Long-grain White Rice (page 81) and Apple Sambal (page 95).
Serves 6

NOTE: The heavier the pot, the lower the heat of the stove plate should be.

CABBAGE AND SWEET TURNIP BREDIE

Prepare this bredie for special occasions.

1 medium spitskop cabbage (curly top)
60 ml (¼ cup) oil
500 g mutton knuckles
500 g thick lamb rib
1 onion, chopped
1 bunch sweet turnips (kohlrabi), peeled and cut into thin, short stalks
250 ml (1 cup) water
5 ml (1 tsp) salt
2.5 ml (½ tsp) cayenne pepper
1 medium potato, peeled and quartered
5 ml (1 tsp) sugar
a pinch turmeric

With a sharp knife, remove the leaves from the cabbage head. In a V pattern, cut away the thick centre stalks of the leaves. Stack in a colander. Wash under slow-running water to remove all sand and dirt. Cut the cabbage into thin strips, toss into cold water and leave to stand. Heat the oil in a large saucepan over medium heat. Add the meat and onion, and cook, covered. Add a little cold water if the meat starts to stick. Allow the meat to braise for about 10 minutes, then add the turnips, water, salt and cayenne pepper. Cook for 5 minutes before adding the potatoes, cabbage, sugar and turmeric. Cook uncovered for a few minutes and give a good stir, making sure that the potatoes are covered by the turnips and cabbage. When the cabbage has dried out, cover the saucepan and reduce the heat. Simmer until done. Serve with Long-grain White Rice (page 81) and Cucumber Salad (page 86).
Serves 6

WATERBLOMMETJIE AND CELERY BREDIE

We call waterblommetjies 'watereendjies', as the plants look like little ducks floating on the water.

1 kg fresh waterblommetjies
60 ml (¼ cup) oil
1.5 kg leg of lamb, cubed
1 large onion, chopped
7.5 ml (1½ tsp) salt
1 green or dried chilli or
a pinch cayenne pepper
1 starseed petal (star anise)
2.5 ml (½ tsp) red masala
2 celery stalks with leaves,
roughly chopped
10 ml (2 tsp) dry breadcrumbs

Remove the tiny flowers from the centre of the waterblommetjies, rinse them in hot water and set aside. Heat the oil slightly, add the meat cubes and onion, and braise until golden brown. Now add the salt, chilli or cayenne pepper, starseed and masala. Reduce the heat and add the waterblommetjies, celery and breadcrumbs. Cook for a further 30 minutes or until the meat is tender and succulent. Remove from the heat and serve piping hot with rice and Apple and Dhania Sambal (page 94).

Serves 6

CABBAGE AND CELERY BREDIE

Turnips can also be added here if you like.

2 marrow bones
1 large onion, chopped
625 ml (2½ cups) water
1 kg brisket, cut into portions
500 g topside, cut into portions
4 medium potatoes, peeled and
quartered
1 large spitskop cabbage (curly top)
¼ bunch celery leaves, torn
1 green chilli, halved
1 starseed petal (star anise)
5 ml (1 tsp) sugar
7.5 ml (1½ tsp) medium-coarse salt
a pinch turmeric

Place the marrow bones in a saucepan together with the onion and 250 ml (1 cup) water and cook, uncovered, for about 15 minutes. Add the well-washed meat with a further 250 ml (1 cup) water. Cover the saucepan and cook until almost dry. Uncover and allow the meat to braise a little until well browned. Add small amounts of water to the meat to prevent it from burning during this process. Add the potatoes with 125 ml (½ cup) water and simmer for 5 minutes before adding the cabbage and the remaining ingredients. Stir thoroughly and cover the saucepan for 5 minutes before uncovering again and cooking until done. Serve with Long-grain White Rice (page 81).

Serves 8

Opposite: Waterblommetjie and Celery Bredie and Cinnamon Rice (page 81)

LAMB TAIL AND CABBAGE BREDIE

A good meal to add to the winter diet sheet!

1 spitskop cabbage (curly top)
3 potatoes, peeled and quartered
60 ml (¼ cup) oil
1 onion, chopped
6 lamb cutlets
4 lambs' tails
125 ml (½ cup) water
5 ml (1 tsp) salt
a pinch turmeric
1 green chilli, chopped
2.5 ml (½ tsp) sugar

Start by separating the cabbage leaves, cutting away the stalks in the centre. Take two leaves at a time, roll and cut into thin ribbon-like shreds, then immerse in a basin of cold water. Now add the potatoes to the cabbage and leave to stand. Heat the oil in a large saucepan, add the onion and braise until golden brown. Add the cutlets and tails, and braise over medium heat until well browned, then add half the water. Meanwhile, rinse the cabbage and potatoes well, divide into two portions so that any sand can be washed out thoroughly, then drain. Place the cabbage, potatoes, meat and remaining ingredients, except the water, in a saucepan. Stir thoroughly. Steam for 10 minutes, pour over the remaining water and simmer for a further 20 minutes. Enjoy with Apple Sambal (page 95) or Apricot and Peach Chutney (page 99) and Long-grain White Rice (page 81).
Serves 6

BROWN LENTIL STEW

Serve with Long-grain White Rice (page 81) and Lemon and Brinjal Atjar (page 97).

500 g (2½ cups) brown lentils
60 ml (¼ cup) oil
2 marrow bones
1 kg stewing beef
1 onion, chopped
½ green pepper, chopped
2.5 ml (½ tsp) crushed chillies or
1 dry red chilli
5 ml (1 tsp) salt
1 tomato, blanched, peeled
and pulped
5 ml (1 tsp) sugar
2 whole cloves
6 allspice
250 ml (1 cup) water

Empty the lentils onto a smooth surface and remove the grit and dust. Place the lentils in a sieve and rinse thoroughly. Now place the lentils in a saucepan with enough boiling water to cover them. Boil for about 45 minutes, strain through a sieve and set aside. Heat the oil in a heavy-based saucepan, add the meat and top with the onion. Braise until browned, about 40 minutes, then add the chopped pepper, chilli and salt. Add the tomato and remaining ingredients plus the lentils. Simmer, covered, over low heat for about 20 minutes.
Serves 6

NOTE: A mixture of cold water and vinegar will rid pots of any cooking odours. Leave the mixture in the pot overnight.

Notes:
• Fast-cook meat only if water has been added to the meat in the pot.
• To prevent the windy aftereffects of eating cabbage, soak it in boiling water for 30 minutes before adding it to the saucepan.
• Roll a lemon between your hands for a few seconds before cutting or squeezing it – it will give you more juice.
• When purchasing trotters and tripe, make sure they are clean. Trotters must be split open between the hooves and the gland removed. Soak for 1 hour before cooking.

LAZY HOUSEWIFE'S GREEN BEAN BREDIE

A lazy housewife doesn't like stringing beans – if possible, buy the Lazy Housewife variety of beans.

1 kg lamb shoulder
500 g thin lamb rib
60 ml (¼ cup) oil
1 medium onion, sliced
500 ml (2 cups) water
1 kg fresh green beans, cut
whichever way you prefer
500 g medium potatoes, peeled and
cut into wedges
7.5 ml (1½ tsp) salt
2.5 ml (½ tsp) sugar
1 red or green chilli, quartered
a pinch ground jeera (cumin)

Cut the meat into suitably-sized pieces. Heat the oil and brown the meat until golden brown before adding the onion and 250 ml (1 cup) water. Simmer until tender, then add the beans and potatoes, salt, sugar and chilli. Stir thoroughly and add the remaining water. Finally add the jeera and cover the saucepan. Simmer on low heat for 20 minutes. Serve with rice and Beetroot and Onion Salad (page 85).

Serves 6

Lazy Housewife's Green Bean Bredie, and Beetroot and Onion Salad (page 85)

BABY CARROT AND TURNIP BREDIE

**3 baby carrots, peeled
and cut into strips
1 bunch baby turnips,
peeled and cut into strips
500 g thin lamb rib
500 g shoulder of mutton, cubed
1 mutton leg chop, cubed
1 onion, chopped
30 ml (2 tbsp) oil
½ chilli, chopped
1 starseed petal (star anise)
5 ml (1 tsp) salt
500 ml (2 cups) water
5 ml (1 tsp) sugar**

Immerse the carrots and turnips in cold water, drain and set aside. Wash and drain the meat. Heat a heavy-based saucepan over medium heat and add the meat and onion. Add the oil and braise until well browned, then add the carrots and cook for 5 minutes. Add the turnips and remaining ingredients, except the sugar. Stir and simmer for about 20 minutes. More water can be added if necessary. Lastly add the sugar, stir thoroughly and remove from the heat. Serve with Long-grain White Rice (page 81) and Carrot and Quince Sambal (page 92).

Serves 6

Baby Carrot and Turnip Curry

BROWN STEW

A winter's day special!

500 g mutton knuckles, cut into
suitably-sized pieces
2 marrow bones
500 g mutton ribs
I kg shoulder of mutton
2.5 ml (½ tsp) red masala
875 ml (3½ cups) water
I large onion, chopped
6 strips green pepper, chopped
I slice tomato
7.5 ml (1½ tsp) medium-coarse salt
5 ml (1 tsp) ground black pepper
I green chilli, chopped
10 ml (2 tsp) fine, dry breadcrumbs
15 ml (1 tbsp) oil
I kg new potatoes, unpeeled

Wash the meat well, drain, season with the masala and set aside. Place the meat, 625 ml (2½ cups) water and the remaining ingredients, except the potatoes, in a shallow, heavy-based saucepan. Cover the saucepan and cook on medium heat until the water has evaporated. The meat should be braised until well browned. Add the whole potatoes and the remaining 250 ml (1 cup) water, enough to cover the stew. Reduce the heat and simmer until done and the sauce is fairly thick. Serve with Long-grain Brown Rice (page 81) and Apple Sambal (page 95).
Sweetcorn Puffs (page 143) and a cup of filter coffee will round off the meal.
Serves 8

DRIED PEA STEW

Another very old recipe, perfect for a wet winter's day.

500 g (2½ cups) dried peas, soaked
and drained
500 ml (2 cups) boiling water
60 ml (¼ cup) oil
I kg stewing beef
I shin bone or 2 marrow bones
I onion, chopped
625 ml (2½ cups) cold water
I dry red chilli
5 ml (1 tsp) cayenne pepper or
crushed chillies
5 ml (1 tsp) salt
I starseed petal (star anise)
2.5 ml (½ tsp) red masala
10 ml (2 tsp) sugar

Boil the peas in the boiling water, drain and set aside. Heat the oil in a heavy-based saucepan over medium heat, add the meat and onion, and cook for a few minutes. Now add 375 ml (1½ cups) cold water and cook until the water has cooked away and the meat has braised to a golden brown. Add a little water to the sizzling saucepan to loosen the meat. Stir well. Allow to braise two to three times until well browned. Add a further 250 ml (1 cup) water and cook, adding the peas and the remaining ingredients. Reduce the heat to low and simmer for 10 minutes. Serve with Long-grain White Rice (page 81) topped with home-made chutney.
Serves 6

NOTES:
- As an alternative, use ox trotter sectioned by the butcher, well washed and cooked with onions into a smoor. Combine with the remaining ingredients and serve with chutney.
- Food such as marrow, pumpkin, drumhead cabbages and watery tomatoes should be cooked, uncovered, until dry enough. Cover when making bredies.

CAPE FARM DUMPLING STEW

A favourite brown stew from my childhood – also known as 'Poor Man's Stew'.

60 ml (¼ cup) oil
1 kg stewing beef or tenderised steak, cubed
1 onion, chopped
750 ml (3 cups) water
5 ml (1 tsp) salt
¼ green pepper, sliced
6 allspice
2 whole cloves
2.5 ml (½ tsp) sugar
5 ml (1 tsp) pepper
4 carrots, peeled, quartered and precooked

DUMPLINGS
250 ml (1 cup) self-raising flour
5 ml (1 tsp) butter or margarine
a pinch ground nutmeg

Heat the oil and braise the meat and onion until golden brown. Add 250 ml (1 cup) water (less if using tenderised steak) to avoid burning. When the meat has browned, add a further 500 ml (2 cups) water; reduce the heat to low. Allow to bubble, then add the salt. To make the dumplings, make a paste with the flour, butter and nutmeg and some of the meat stock, cooled, and stir quickly. Drop spoonfuls of paste into the stew, add the remaining ingredients, except the carrots, and simmer until the dumplings are done. Now add the carrots to enhance the flavour and cook until done. Do not allow to cook dry. Serve immediately with rice and Quince Sambal (page 94).
Serves 6

Cape Farm Dumpling Stew

OXTAIL AND SUGAR BEAN STEW

The oxtail needs to be cooked for a long time to ensure that it is tender.

500 g (2½ cups) sugar beans
500 g brisket, cubed
I small oxtail, sectioned
I medium onion, chopped
560 ml (2¼ cups) water
30 ml (2 tbsp) oil
¼ red or green pepper, sliced
I small tomato, blanched, peeled
and pulped
7.5 ml (1½ tsp) salt
2.5 ml (½ tsp) dried thyme
I clove garlic, crushed
I starseed petal (star anise)

To swell the beans, soak and leave for 3 hours, or overnight, in water. First cook in boiling water for 30 minutes, then drain. Add a pinch of bicarbonate of soda while cooking beans to soften them, then cook in more water until tender, then drain again. Some of the stock can be retained for the meat. Be careful not to boil the beans for too long, or they will turn into soup instead of stew. Heat a heavy-based saucepan over medium heat. Spread the brisket and oxtail on the base of the saucepan. Top with the onion and 500 ml (2 cups) water, and cook until all the water has cooked away. Add the oil, braise, then add 60 ml (¼ cup) water and cook until all the meat is tender. More water can be added if the meat is still tough and needs further cooking. Add the beans and remaining ingredients. Stir through and simmer slowly for 10 minutes. Serve with white rice and Apricot and Peach Chutney (page 99).

Serves 6

NOTE: Instead of soaking sugar beans overnight to swell them, pour boiling water over them and leave to stand in the sun for a couple of hours.

GRANDMA'S SAGO STEW

I grew up with my grandma and spent much of my childhood helping her in the kitchen – this is one of her special winter stews.

500 g chump chops
500 g mutton flat ribs
60 ml (¼ cup) oil
I onion, chopped
about 375 ml (1½ cups) water
7.5 ml (1½ tsp) salt
3 medium potatoes, peeled and sliced
185 ml (¾ cup) sago, soaked in
water for 2 hours
½ red or green pepper, chopped
5 allspice
3 whole cloves
½ red or green chilli, torn
5 ml (1 tsp) black or white pepper
a pinch grated nutmeg
I starseed petal (star anise)
juice of ½ lemon
2 sprigs celery, torn
60 ml (¼ cup) chopped parsley

Cut the meat into suitably-sized pieces. Wash thoroughly and drain. Heat the oil over medium heat until very warm. First add the meat, then the onion and braise until golden brown and dry. Add a little water to brown the onion, then add 250 ml (1 cup) water, salt and potatoes. Spread the meat and potatoes evenly in the pot and cook for 10 minutes. Reduce the heat to low. Top the meat and potatoes with sago and add 125 ml (½ cup) water. It is important that you do not stir at this stage – the sago must not be disturbed on top or it will stick to the pot. Cover and steam for 15 minutes. Add the remaining spices, lemon juice, celery and lastly the parsley. Stir the mixture lightly once or twice while simmering for 20 minutes Enjoy this meal with home-made chutney.

Serves 6

LAMB TROTTER AND TOMATO STEW

To prepare the trotters, carefully slit the hoof and remove the tiny gland if this has not already been done, or ask your butcher to do it for you. Soak for 30 minutes in lukewarm, salted water.

12 lamb trotters, prepared (see above)
60 ml (¼ cup) oil
1 onion, chopped
500 g tomatoes, blanched and peeled
10 ml (2 tsp) salt
10 ml (2 tsp) tomato paste
30 ml (2 tbsp) sugar
1 starseed petal (star anise)
½ green chilli, halved
¼ green pepper, chopped

Cook the prepared trotters in water for 2 hours in a saucepan or 1 hour in a pressure cooker. Heat the oil over medium heat and add the onion. Braise until golden brown, then add the trotters, tomatoes and salt, and cook for 10 minutes. When adding the trotters, do not add the stock they were boiled in unless necessary. Reduce the heat and add the remaining ingredients. Cook, uncovered, for 10–20 minutes. Delicious served with Long-grain White Rice (page 81) and Apple Sambal (page 95).

Serves 6

CAPE CARROT STEW

This stew is traditionally served at funerals.

60 ml (¼ cup) oil
1 onion, chopped
500 g shoulder of mutton, washed and drained
500 g mutton knuckles, washed and drained
2 marrow bones, washed and drained
2 bunches young carrots, peeled and sliced
3 medium potatoes, peeled and quartered
5 ml (1 tsp) salt
4 whole cloves
4 allspice
½ red or green chilli, chopped
5 ml (1 tsp) sugar
a pinch grated nutmeg
2.5 ml (½ tsp) white or black pepper
60 ml (¼ cup) chopped parsley

Heat the oil in a saucepan over medium heat. Add the onion and meat, and cover. Allow the meat to braise, then add small quantities of water until the meat is sufficiently browned. Now add the carrots, potatoes, salt, cloves, allspice, chilli and 250 ml (1 cup) water. Simmer for 10 minutes, stirring occasionally, and reduce the heat. Now add the sugar, nutmeg, pepper and parsley and simmer until done. Frozen or fresh peas can be added to this dish if desired. If less gravy is preferred, make the carrot stew into a bredie by cooking until semi-dry.

Serves 5

LAMB AND PUMPKIN STEW

The secret ingredient in this tasty stew is the ginger, which enhances the flavour of the pumpkin. Make sure the pumpkin has a rich, orange skin.

60 ml (¼ cup) oil
3 marrow bones
375 ml (1½ cups) cold water
500 g shoulder of mutton
500 g mutton knuckles
1 onion, chopped
1 red or green chilli, torn
10 ml (2 tsp) salt
10 ml (2 tsp) brown or white sugar
1 kg pumpkin, peeled, washed and cubed
1 walnut-sized piece of fresh ginger, crushed
a pinch turmeric
½ red or green pepper, sliced
1 starseed petal (star anise)

Cook this dish uncovered. Heat the oil in a heavy-based saucepan on medium heat, add the marrow bones and 250 ml (1 cup) water, and cook for 15 minutes. Add the rest of the meat that has been cut to the desired size. Top it with the onion. Add a further 125 ml (½ cup) water. Simmer until dry, making sure that it does not burn. Now add 60 ml (¼ cup) water two to three times until the meat is medium brown. Add the chilli, salt, sugar and pumpkin. Stir thoroughly. If the pumpkin draws its own water, do not add extra water. Cook for 15 minutes, then toss in the ginger, turmeric and sliced pepper. Stir and simmer over low heat unless it needs drying out. Enjoy this meal with Long-grain White Rice (page 81) and homemade chutney.

Serves 6

Lamb and Pumpkin Stew

CHAPTER 7

RICE, VEGETABLES AND SALADS

One of the most important dishes on the Malay table, rice can be served with almost any meal! Vegetables are often smoored (braised in oil or fat) and salads are preferred accompaniments to curries and grills.

BRAISED TOMATO

A warm dish that goes well with fish.

30 ml (2 tbsp) oil
1 medium onion, sliced
4 tomatoes, blanched, peeled and chopped
3 slices green pepper
sugar to taste
2.5 ml (½ tsp) leaf masala

Heat the oil in a pan and braise the onion. Add the tomatoes, green pepper with sugar to taste and the masala. Stir-fry for about 10 minutes until the tomato is tender. Serve with a fish, chicken or meat dish of your choice.
Serves 4

NOTE: Blanch tomatoes by plunging into boiling water to loosen the skins.

SPICY CARROTS AND GEM SQUASH

The spicy tang of nutmeg enhances the understated flavours of the carrots and squash. Gem squash halves can also be cooked until tender and filled with early garden peas and corn kernels.

½ bunch baby carrots, peeled and sliced
3 young gem squashes, halved and pips removed
2.5 ml (½ tsp) salt
nut of butter or margarine
a pinch ground or grated nutmeg

In a large saucepan, steam the carrots and squash together in a little boiling water with the salt and butter or margarine. When softened, serve sprinkled with the nutmeg.
Serves 6

CINNAMON PUMPKIN

The perfect vegetable to serve alongside a mutton stew.

125 ml (½ cup) cold water
500 g pumpkin, peeled and thickly wedged
30 ml (2 tbsp) soft butter
2 cinnamon sticks or 5 ml (1 tsp) ground cinnamon
5 ml (1 tsp) soft brown sugar
5 ml (1 tsp) white sugar

Pour the water into a heavy-based saucepan and spread the pumpkin over the base in about two layers. Top with the remaining ingredients and slow-steam on low heat until soft.
Serves 6

Clockwise from the top: Spicy Carrots and Gem Squash, Cinnamon Pumpkin and Braised Tomato

SAVOURY RICE

A meal in itself or serve as a side dish – brown rice flavoured with chillies to give it added zest.

500 g (2½ cups) uncooked long-grain brown rice
15 ml (1 tbsp) salt
30 ml (2 tbsp) oil
2 pieces stick cinnamon
1 large onion, sliced
30 ml (2 tbsp) soft butter
½ red or green pepper, shredded
125 ml (½ cup) celery leaves, torn
1 x 410 g tin whole-kernel corn, drained
2 small green chillies, torn
2.5 ml (½ tsp) red masala
2.5 ml (½ tsp) dried thyme

125 g screw noodles (optional)
5 ml (1 tsp) oil (if using noodles)

Boil the rice in water with 10 ml (2 tsp) salt. Strain and steam in a colander over rapidly boiling water. Heat the oil and cinnamon in a saucepan. Toss in the onion and stir-fry until golden brown; set aside. Heat the butter and stir-fry the shredded pepper and celery leaves for a few minutes. Add the rice, onion mixture, corn and chillies. Transfer to a heavy-based saucepan. Add the masala and thyme. Remove from the heat and place in a warming drawer. If using noodles, cook in rapidly boiling water with the remaining salt and the oil for 15 minutes. When *al dente*, drain and add to the rice.
Serves 4–6

KHITCHRI RICE

To save on cooking time, soak the red lentils in water for about an hour beforehand.

500 g (2½ cups) uncooked long-grain white rice
1 litre (4 cups) boiling water
10 ml (2 tsp) salt
60 g (¼ cup) red lentils
4 pieces stick cinnamon

Boil the rice in salted, boiling water with the lentils and cinnamon for about 20 minutes or until done. Drain, rinse and steam on medium heat for 10–15 minutes. Serve hot.
Serves 4–6

Khitchri Rice and Savoury Rice

CINNAMON RICE

Cinnamon rice is a delicious accompaniment to any fish, meat or chicken dish.

1.5 litres (6 cups) water
a pinch turmeric
500 g (2½ cups) uncooked long-grain white rice
2 pieces stick cinnamon
15 ml (1 tbsp) salt

In a deep saucepan, boil the water and add the turmeric, then the remaining ingredients, and allow to cook rapidly for 10 minutes. Turn down the heat and cook slowly until the rice is tender. Strain and steam in a colander over rapidly boiling water for 10 minutes.
Serves 4–6

LONG-GRAIN WHITE OR BROWN RICE

No curry or bredie would be complete without rice.

500 g (2½ cups) uncooked long-grain white or brown rice
15 ml (1 tbsp) medium-coarse salt
1 litre (4 cups) boiling water

Steam white rice for 20 minutes and brown rice for 25–30 minutes in a colander over boiling salted water. The bottom of the colander should not touch the water. This basic recipe can be livened up by adding a piece of stick cinnamon during steaming.
Serves 6

SWEET SULTANA YELLOW RICE

Instead of using cinnamon, add a few drops of vanilla essence with 2.5 ml (½ tsp) ground cardamom.

500 g (2½ cups) parboiled long-grain white rice
1 litre (4 cups) boiling water
2.5 ml (½ tsp) turmeric
4 small pieces stick cinnamon
10 ml (2 tsp) salt
30 ml (2 tbsp) butter
60 ml (¼ cup) sultanas
15 ml (1 tbsp) sugar

Add the rice to the boiling water, then add the turmeric, cinnamon and salt. Boil for 20 minutes, adding more water if necessary. When the rice is tender, strain under cold running water. Steam the rice in a colander over 2 litres (8 cups) rapidly boiling water for 10 minutes. Return the rice to the pan on low heat and add the butter. Finally add the sultanas and sugar, stir well, steam until the sultanas are a little plump, and serve hot.
Serve 4–6

BRAISED BROWN RICE

A wholesome alternative to white rice.

500 g (2½ cups) uncooked brown rice
1 litre (4 cups) boiling water
10 ml (2 tsp) salt
10 ml (2 tsp) oil
1 small onion, sliced
1 piece stick cinnamon

Cook the rice in rapidly boiling, salted water for 10 minutes, then simmer for a further 10 minutes. Strain and steam in a colander over boiling water. Heat the oil in a saucepan and add the onion and stick cinnamon. Fry the onion until golden brown. Add the steamed rice to the onion mixture, mix well and allow to heat through for about 5 minutes. Serve hot.
Serves 6

MALAYAN CAULIFLOWER

Traditional cauliflower cheese seasoned with masala makes this a hot favourite.

1 medium cauliflower
2.5 ml (½ tsp) medium-coarse salt
10 ml (2 tsp) cornflour
375 ml (1½ cups) milk
60 g (¼ cup) butter
30 ml (2 tbsp) fresh double cream
60 g (¼ cup) finely grated Parmesan or Cheddar cheese
a pinch leaf masala

Wash the cauliflower under slow-running cold water. Steam the whole cauliflower in a little water over low heat with 2.5 ml (½ tsp) salt for about 20 minutes or until just tender. Carefully lift the cauliflower from the saucepan with slotted spoons and place on an ovenproof platter. Blend the cornflour and milk into a paste with a pinch of salt. Heat the butter in a shallow saucepan. Add the cornflour paste and stir until smooth, then stir in the cream, blending well. Remove from the heat and allow to cool. Pour the sauce over the cauliflower, top with the cheese and masala, and bake on the middle shelf of the oven at 200 °C until golden brown.
Serves 4

NOTES:
- A few drops of lemon juice added to cauliflower or potatoes while boiling will whiten them.
- It is healthier to steam vegetables than to boil them.

GLAZED CARROTS

These are always popular served with stews or bredies.

1 kg baby carrots, scraped and washed
250 ml (1 cup) water
5 ml (1 tsp) golden syrup
2.5 ml (½ tsp) salt
1 piece stick cinnamon
5 ml (1 tsp) soft brown sugar
5 ml (1 tsp) white sugar

Place the carrots in a shallow saucepan and cover with the water. Add the remaining ingredients and steam over medium heat, covered, for 5 minutes. Remove the lid and steam until the carrots are tender and semi-dry.
Serves 6

MIXED VEGETABLE SMOOR

Use any vegetables in season – especially good are carrots, beans, peas, corn kernels and potatoes.

60 g (¼ cup) butter
2 baby leeks, sliced in rounds
500 g mixed vegetables, diced
a pinch dried thyme
a pinch dried oregano
a pinch dried sweet basil

Heat the butter and stir-fry the leeks until brown. Add the remaining vegetables and herbs, and cook quickly until just tender. Remove from the heat and serve immediately.
Serves 4

CABBAGE SMOOR

30 ml (2 tbsp) oil
1 small onion, thinly sliced
1 small spitskop cabbage
(curly top), shredded
2.5 ml (½ tsp) medium-coarse salt
2.5 ml (½ tsp) crushed chillies
5 ml (1 tsp) white sugar
a pinch turmeric
2.5 ml (½ tsp) caraway seeds

Heat the oil in a skillet or pan and stir-fry the onion until golden brown. Add the remaining ingredients and stir-fry until just tender – be careful not to overcook. Remove from the heat and serve immediately.
Serves 4

BAKED PUMPKIN

Serve with your favourite roast.

1 kg pumpkin, peeled and cut
into thick slices
15 ml (1 tbsp) melted butter
15 ml (1 tbsp) soft brown sugar
15 ml (1 tbsp) ground cinnamon

Place the pumpkin on a well-greased baking sheet, pour over the butter and sprinkle over the sugar and cinnamon. Bake on the middle shelf at 180 °C for 25 minutes.
Serves 6

MASALA CHIPS

Liven up potato chips with a tang of masala and turmeric.

500 g medium potatoes, peeled and
cut into paper-thin rounds
a pinch coarse salt
a pinch leaf masala
a pinch turmeric
oil for deep-frying

Season the potato rounds with the salt, masala and turmeric and leave to stand for a few minutes. Deep-fry in hot oil until golden brown and serve immediately with your favourite fish dish.
Serves 4

STEWED SWEET POTATOES

The combination of the sweet potatoes, coconut and cinnamon makes this a traditional Malay side dish. Buy borrie sweet potatoes (with the red skin) if you can – they are sweeter and less watery than white-skinned sweet potatoes.

1 kg borrie sweet potatoes, peeled
and cut into thick rounds
250 ml (1 cup) water
60 ml (¼ cup) desiccated coconut
250 ml (1 cup) yellow sugar
60 g (¼ cup) butter
4 pieces stick cinnamon

Toss the sweet potatoes into cold, salted water to prevent discoloration. Drain and set aside. Heat a heavy-based saucepan over low heat and add the water. When hot, add the drained sweet potatoes, coconut, sugar, butter and cinnamon. Cover and cook for about 20 minutes – do not stir. Uncover the pan and cook for a further 20 minutes until the sweet potatoes are soft. If necessary, add more sugar to taste. Stir only once or twice. Serve immediately while still piping hot.
Serves 6

Green Bean Smoor, Masala Chips (page 83) and Stewed Sweet Potatoes (page 83)

GREEN BEAN SMOOR

The word 'smoor' means 'braised' – the Malays' favourite way of preparing vegetables by braising them in oil or fat.

15 ml (1 tbsp) oil
2 baby leeks, sliced in rounds
1 x 410 g tin stubbed green beans, drained
2.5 ml (½ tsp) medium-coarse salt
2.5 ml (½ tsp) crushed chillies
5 ml (1 tsp) white sugar
a pinch ground jeera (cumin)

Heat the oil and stir-fry the leeks until brown. Add the remaining ingredients and cook quickly until just tender. Remove from the heat and serve immediately.
Serves 4

BEETROOT AND ONION SALAD

A favourite Cape Malay salad – we eat it nearly every day.

1 bunch baby beetroot
7.5 ml (1½ tsp) salt
1 large onion, thinly sliced
2.5 ml (½ tsp) ground black pepper or 1 piece green chilli, chopped
7.5 ml (1½ tsp) sugar
60 ml (4 tbsp) brown vinegar

Chop off the beetroot stalks. Boil the beetroot covered in water until soft. This could be quite a lengthy process if you don't have a pressure cooker, so make sure you do it ahead of time. Allow to cool, then peel and slice the beetroot thinly. Add the salt to the onion and squeeze in one hand a few times. Toss into boiling water, stir briefly, strain and add to the beetroot. Add the pepper or chilli and sugar. Pour the vinegar over. This salad can be made a couple of hours in advance and refrigerated or served straight away. It looks best served in a pretty glass bowl.
Serves 4

SEPTEMBER CRESS

A winter salad – watercress and kumquats are normally only available at this time.

1 queen pineapple, peeled and grated
4 young carrots, peeled and grated
125 g (½ cup) small noodles, cooked and drained
1 young lettuce, torn
½ bunch young watercress leaves
500 g kumquats, pitted
few stubs celery stalk and leaves
10 Californian nuts, halved
15 ml (1 tbsp) mayonnaise

Combine the grated pineapple and carrots, and leave to stand for 20 minutes. Add the remaining ingredients and mix well. Chill for 30 minutes before serving.
Serves 4

SULTAN'S COLESLAW

A coleslaw fit for a sultan!

front end of a small spitskop cabbage (curly top)
1 x 225 g tin peach slices, halved and drained (syrup retained)
30 ml (2 tbsp) mayonnaise
3 slices red or green pepper, finely chopped
1 x 225 g tin choice peas, drained
125 ml (½ cup) whole-kernel corn, drained
6 macadamia nuts, blanched, peeled and quartered

Shred, blanch and drain the cabbage. Refresh in the refrigerator for 30 minutes. Mix together the peach syrup, mayonnaise and chopped peppers. Add the cabbage and the remaining ingredients, and allow to steep and chill for about 20 minutes before serving.
Serves 6

CUCUMBER SALAD

Another favourite salad in our house, often served with our Sunday meal. It's a cool companion to bredies and stews.

1 medium cucumber
125 ml (½ cup) brown vinegar
1 green chilli, sliced
sugar to taste

Cut off cucumber ends and rub these against either end of the cucumber to prevent bitterness. Peel and run fork tines lengthwise down cucumber, then slice thinly. Place in a bowl and add vinegar, chilli and sugar to taste. Chill before serving.
Serves 4

FETA CHEESE AND GHERKIN SALAD

4 crisp lettuce leaves, torn
1 small jar baby gherkins, drained
10 black olives
6 yellow cocktail onions
1 small onion, thinly sliced into rings
½ English cucumber, thinly sliced
1 firm avocado, peeled, cut into wedges and dipped into juice of 1 lemon
1 firm tomato, cut into wedges
10 Californian nuts, shelled and halved

GARNISH
10 blocks feta cheese
60 ml (¼ cup) mung bean sprouts
ground black pepper to taste

Arrange the lettuce in a shallow bowl. Mix the remaining ingredients and pile onto the lettuce leaves. Garnish with the feta cheese, sprouts and pepper. Chill for about 20 minutes and serve.
Serves 4–6

Sultan's Coleslaw with Tomato and Dhania Salad (page 89)

TUNA SALAD

You could serve this with Quick Onion Bread (page 136) or toast for an easy supper or a light lunch.

3 slices English cucumber, chopped
1 small fresh tomato, cubed
2.5 ml (½ tsp) masala
125 ml (½ cup) wheat rice (stampkoring),
cooked for 30 minutes and strained
1 leek, chopped
2.5 ml (½ tsp) ground black pepper
30 ml (2 tbsp) mayonnaise
3 young lettuce leaves, shredded
2 x 185 g tins light meat tuna, drained

Mix all the ingredients together lightly, except the lettuce and tuna. Line a deep glass bowl with the lettuce leaves. Arrange the salad and tuna on the lettuce leaves and chill before serving.
Serves 6

CRAYFISH SALAD

Reserve this elegant starter for special occasions, or serve at a brunch as a mystery ball, wrapped in young lettuce leaves and held together with toothpicks.

2 crayfish tails
a pinch cayenne pepper
15 ml (1 tbsp) mayonnaise
1 slice red pepper, chopped
3 drops lemon juice
2.5 ml (½ tsp) white pepper
4–6 lettuce leaves
tiny mint leaves for garnish

Steam the crayfish tails in salted water for 20 minutes and chill for 1 hour. Shred and toss into a glass bowl. Add the cayenne pepper and leave to stand for about 3 minutes. Now add the mayonnaise, peppers and lemon juice. Arrange the lettuce leaves in bowls, spoon in the crayfish mixture, and decorate with the mint leaves.
Serves 4 as a starter or 2 as a meal

BAKED BEAN SALAD

Perfect for those in a hurry!

1 x 410 g tin baked beans, juice retained
2 baby leeks or spring onions, chopped
10 ml (2 tsp) chopped green pepper
3 slices English cucumber, chopped
10 ml (2 tsp) chopped parsley
10 ml (2 tsp) brown vinegar
sugar to taste

Mix together all the ingredients, adding sugar to taste. Chill for about 30 minutes before serving.
Serves 4

CHILLED SHRIMP SALAD

1 x 454 g packet peeled shrimps
a pinch cayenne pepper
60 ml (¼ cup) mayonnaise
1 x 130 g jar white cocktail onions, drained
very young lettuce leaves

Cook the shrimps according to the instructions on the packet. Lightly mix together the shrimps, pepper, mayonnaise and onions. Arrange the lettuce leaves in a shallow bowl. Place scoops of shrimp mixture onto each leaf.
Serves 4–6

TOMATO AND DHANIA SALAD

A salad for the adventurous eater!

1 large onion, sliced
3 firm tomatoes, cut into cubes
1 small green chilli, chopped
60 ml (¼ cup) chopped green dhania (coriander) leaves
125 ml (¼ cup) vinegar
sugar to taste

Rub the sliced onion with a little salt, toss into boiling water, strain and squeeze dry – this prevents bitterness. Mix all the ingredients together with sugar to taste. Chill and serve.
Serves 4

CHAPTER 8

SAMBALS, ATJARS AND SAUCES

A sambal consists of grated vegetables or fruit, seasoned with salt, chillies or vinegar. An atjar is a relish made from sliced vegetables or fruit, flavoured with spices and covered with vinegar or oil.

CHILLI SAUCE

Fiery stuff – unless you're tough, have a glass of water close at hand!

1 x 410 g tin tomato purée
45 ml (3 tbsp) crushed, dried chilli
1 x 65 g tin tomato paste
15 ml (1 tbsp) oil
30 ml (2 tbsp) white sugar, or to taste

Mix all the ingredients together, adding sugar to taste. The sauce can be served immediately but will last indefinitely in an airtight jar stored in the fridge.

PICCALILLI

My prize recipe – not even my children know how to make this! It's a real success at a bazaar if made the right way. Delight your family and serve alongside corned beef and roasts.

2 bunches carrots, peeled
1 medium cauliflower
2 x 410 g tins sliced green beans, drained
1 small jar gherkins, drained and thickly sliced
50 ml (3 tbsp) dry mustard
10 ml (2 tsp) cayenne pepper
10 ml (2 tsp) turmeric
30 ml (2 tbsp) oil
750 ml (3 cups) cold water
5 ml (1 tsp) salt
3 x 750 ml bottles white vinegar
60 ml (¼ cup) cornflour
15 ml (1 tbsp) mustard seeds
1 starseed petal (star anise)
625 ml (2½ cups) sugar

Cut the carrots into stubs. Pour boiling water over and steam for 5 minutes. Drain and transfer to a basin. Prepare the cauliflower in the same manner, but do not make the florets too small. Do not overcook the vegetables, as it will make the piccalilly soggy. Add the drained green beans and gherkins. Mix the mustard, cayenne pepper, turmeric and oil with 375 ml (1½ cups) cold water and salt. Boil the vinegar and stir in the mustard paste. Make a paste from the cornflour and remaining water, and stir into the boiling vinegar mixture. Continue stirring, reduce the heat and add the starseed petal and sugar. Remove from the heat and, when cold, pour over the vegetables. Leave to draw in the fridge for half a day, then bottle in airtight jars – it will last indefinitely in the fridge. Serve with roasts or grills, or even on a sandwich with cold meats.
Makes 4–5 x 750 g jars

CARROT AND QUINCE SAMBAL

A must with curried dishes and good with fish.

1 ripe quince, peeled, cored and coarsely grated
a pinch salt
2 carrots, peeled and finely grated
juice of ½ lemon
5 ml (1 tsp) sugar

Add the salt to the quince and leave to stand for a good while. Press out all the liquid, place in a bowl and add the remaining ingredients.

Note:
• Sambals should be eaten straight away. Atjars can be stored in airtight jars indefinitely.
• Unless indicated, all these recipes serve 4–6 people.

Chilli Sauce (top left), Piccalilli (top right) and Lemon and Brinjal Atjar (page 97)

APPLE AND DHANIA SAMBAL

One of my favourites!

**2 Golden Delicious apples, peeled,
cored and grated
juice of 1 lemon
30 ml (2 tbsp) green dhania
(coriander) leaves
a pinch salt
2 cloves garlic, crushed
1 green chilli, chopped
sugar to taste (optional)**

Soak the apples in the the lemon juice for a while. Chop the dhania leaves coarsely and add to the apples, together with the remaining ingredients. If desired, add sugar to taste.

CARROT AND PINEAPPLE SAMBAL

A cool and refreshing sambal, the perfect accompaniment to a hot meal.

**4 carrots, peeled and
coarsely grated
½ pineapple, peeled and grated
15 ml (1 tbsp) blackcurrants
a few almonds, quartered
5 ml (1 tsp) sugar**

Mix together all the ingredients. Leave to stand for 30 minutes and, if preferred, drain away some of the juice so that it is almost dry.

QUINCE SAMBAL

This is a traditional recipe. The quince may change colour about an hour after preparing this, but don't be put off – it'll still taste lovely!

**1 quince, peeled, cored and grated
a pinch salt
1 green chilli, chopped or
a pinch cayenne pepper
juice of ½ lemon
sugar to taste**

Add the salt to the grated quince and leave to stand for a while. Drain well, then add the remaining ingredients with sugar to taste. Chill for a few minutes before serving.

DHANIA SAMBAL

**1 bunch green dhania (coriander) leaves
½ green pepper, chopped
2 green chillies, chopped
2 cloves garlic, crushed
a pinch medium-coarse salt
juice of 1 lemon
sugar to taste (optional)**

Wash the dhania leaves under cold, running water, and chop coarsely. Add the remaining ingredients plus sugar to taste, if desired, and serve.

TOMATO AND MINT SAMBAL

Mint leaves have a very strong flavour, so remember to chop them finely.

2 firm tomatoes, diced
4 fresh mint leaves, finely chopped
1 green chilli, chopped
30 ml (2 tbsp) vinegar
sugar to taste

Mix together all the ingredients, adding sugar to taste. Chill and serve.

APPLE AND ROOT GINGER SAMBAL

This has a very strong flavour – you'll only need a small amount with your bredie or stew. If preferred, leave out the chilli for a milder but still tasty sambal.

2 soft apples, peeled, cored
and grated
a pinch salt
60 g (¼ cup) fresh ginger, crushed
1 clove garlic, crushed
1 green chilli, crushed
juice of 1 lemon
sugar to taste (optional)

Add the salt to the apples and leave a while before draining. Add the ginger, garlic and chilli (if using), squeezing the lemon juice over last, and add sugar to taste, if desired.

APPLE SAMBAL

I pity those on diet – once you start eating this with your curry, you won't be able to stop!

2 hard apples, peeled and grated
juice of 1 lemon
1 clove garlic, crushed
1 small green chilli, chopped
sugar to taste (optional)

Toss the grated apple in the lemon juice, then add the remaining ingredients. If the apples are sour, add a little sugar. Chill and serve.

CARROT AND CHILLI SAMBAL

The carrots make this sambal fairly juicy.

3 young carrots, peeled and grated
a pinch salt
1 green chilli, chopped
2.5 ml (½ tsp) sugar
15 ml (1 tbsp) blackcurrants
sugar to taste (optional)

Sprinkle a little salt over the grated carrots and drain after a while. Add the remaining ingredients plus sugar to taste, if desired. Chill for a few minutes, then serve immediately.

KIWI SAMBAL

A fruity sambal with a refreshing taste.

4 kiwi fruit, peeled and pulped
1 clove garlic, crushed
10 ml (2 tsp) lemon juice
sugar to taste

Mix together all ingredients, adding sugar to taste. Chill and serve.

Kiwi Sambal and Tomato and Mint Sambal (page 95)

PINEAPPLE AND PEACH MAYONNAISE

A real winner – serve as a relish with roasts or grills.

1 x 385 g tin peaches in thick syrup,
drained (syrup retained)
1 medium pineapple, peeled,
then grated or chopped
200 g (1 cup) small noodles, cooked
1 x 250 g jar mayonnaise
3 slices red pepper, finely chopped

Cube or cut the peaches into strips and place in a mixing bowl. Add the pineapple, noodles and mayonnaise. Now gently blend in the peach syrup and stir lightly. Garnish with the chopped peppers. Serve with a roast or with Devilled Chicken (page 32) or Potroast Leg of Lamb (page 40).

MALAYAN RELISH

A colourful and tangy sauce that goes especially well with curries.

3 firm tomatoes
6 mint leaves, chopped
a pinch salt
a pinch paprika
1 baby onion, chopped
15 ml (1 tbsp) sugar

Blanch, peel and pulp the tomatoes. Combine with the remaining ingredients, mix thoroughly and serve straight away.

CREAM OF MUSHROOM SAUCE

A lovely accompaniment to roasts and grills.

5 ml (1 tsp) cake flour
500 ml (2 cups) milk or thin cream
15 ml (1 tsp) melted butter
a pinch salt
a pinch pepper
1 x 250 g tin button mushrooms,
drained and halved

Make a paste with the flour and milk by slowly cooking the milk over medium heat and stirring in the flour. Add the remaining ingredients, stirring in the mushrooms last. Serve immediately while hot.

TARTAR SAUCE

A must with grilled or fried fish.

3 slices red or green pepper,
chopped
30 ml (2 tbsp) olives, chopped
a pinch paprika
250 ml (1 cup) mayonnaise

juice of 1 lemon
1 small onion, finely chopped

Mix together all the ingredients and chill for a few minutes in the fridge. Serve immediately.

LEMON AND BRINJAL ATJAR

One of the best-loved Muslim atjar recipes.

15 ml (1 tbsp) medium-coarse salt
6 thick-skinned lemons, wedged,
pitted and lightly squeezed
60 ml (¼ cup) methi, soaked for
2 hours in boiling water
750 ml (3 cups) oil
10 ml (2 tsp) turmeric
30 ml (2 tbsp) crushed chilli
5 ml (1 tsp) red masala
5 ml (1 tsp) gharum masala
1 starseed petal (star anise)
10 ml (2 tsp) sugar
600 g baby brinjals, wedged and
soaked in salt water
500 ml (2 cups) boiling water

Sprinkle 7.5 ml (1½ tsp) salt over the lemon wedges and leave to stand overnight. Pour boiling water over the lemons, set aside for 30 minutes, then rinse and drain. Pour the methi into a fine sieve and rinse, drain, then add to very little boiling water and boil for 5 minutes; strain and allow to cool. Heat the oil to almost boiling point in a heavy-based saucepan, remove from the heat, add the methi, 5 ml (1 tsp) salt, 7.5 ml (1½ tsp) turmeric, chilli, remaining spices, and sugar. Stir well and set aside. Add the brinjal wedges to the remaining 2.5 ml (½ tsp) turmeric, the boiling water and the remaining 2.5 ml (½ tsp) salt. Cook rapidly for 5 minutes, then slowly for 10 minutes. Remove from the heat, drain and allow to cool. Layer the lemons and brinjals in a large dish. Add the hot oil and spice mixture, cover and leave to draw in the fridge for three days. Bottle in airtight jars and store in the fridge.

Notes:
• Tinned apricots can be used instead of peaches when making Pineapple and Peach Mayonnaise (page 96).
• Atjars should be stored in airtight jars in the fridge.
• If using green dhania (coriander) leaves instead of mint, use double the amount.
• A dried orange peel in the teapot gives a delicious flavour when making tea.

LEMON AND KUMQUAT ATJAR

A fresh-tasting, all-round atjar; ideal with a breyani or curry.

**10 ml (2 tsp) methi, soaked for
2 hours in boiling water
500 g lemons, quartered and pitted
2.5 ml (½ tsp) salt
500 g kumquats, pitted and cut
into wedges
750 ml (3 cups) oil
10 ml (2 tsp) turmeric
10 ml (2 tsp) tandoori masala**

**5 ml (1 tsp) gharum masala
1 starseed petal (star anise)**

Pour the methi into a fine sieve and rinse, drain, then add to very little boiling water and boil for 5 minutes; strain and leave to cool. Steam the lemons for 5 minutes in a little water with the salt. Drain and set aside. Pour boiling water over the kumquats and steam for 2 minutes. Drain and add to the lemons. Heat the oil to just before boiling point and add the spices. Remove from the heat and allow to cool completely. Pour over the lemons and kumquats, and store in an airtight jar in the fridge.

CABBAGE, CARROT AND BEAN ATJAR

As you use the atjar and the oil runs low, add extra oil to cover the vegetables.

**15 ml (1 tbsp) methi, soaked for 2 hours
in boiling water
1 small spitskop cabbage (curly top),
shredded after discarding thick stalks
500 g baby carrots, peeled
and stubbed
1 x 410 g tin stubbed green beans,
drained
750 ml (3 cups) oil
7.5 ml (1½ tsp) medium-coarse salt**

**10 ml (2 tsp) mustard seeds
10 ml (2 tsp) brown sugar
5 ml (1 tsp) gharum masala
5 ml (1 tsp) cayenne pepper
1 starseed petal (star anise)**

Pour the methi into a fine sieve and rinse, drain, then add to very little boiling water and boil for 5 minutes; strain and leave to cool. Wash the cabbage and carrots in a colander under cold water. Transfer to a saucepan of 750 ml (3 cups) boiling salted water. Slow-steam in the water for 5 minutes. Remove from the heat and drain. Transfer to a large, shallow porcelain dish and leave to cool before adding the green beans. Heat the oil and add the spices. Stir a few times, maintaining a low heat. Remove from the heat and allow to cool. Add to the vegetables, so that they are completely covered with oil; allow to draw in the fridge for a few days. Bottle and store in the fridge.

APRICOT AND PEACH CHUTNEY

A fruity chutney always goes well with a bredie or stew.

30 ml (2 tbsp) coriander seeds
10 ml (2 tsp) oil
1 medium onion, chopped
750 ml (3 cups) brown vinegar
1 x 450 g tin apricot jam
1 x 450 g tin peach jam
125 ml (½ cup) sugar
15 ml (1 tbsp) dried, crushed chilli
250 ml (1 cup) prepared fruit chutney
15 ml (1 tbsp) crushed garlic
5 ml (1 tsp) salt
1 starseed petal (star anise)

Scorch the coriander seeds in 5 ml (1 tsp) oil in a heavy-based pan and remove from the heat the moment they change colour. Grind in a mill or crush with a rolling pin, and set aside. Scorch the onion in 5 ml (1 tsp) oil and add to the coriander. Heat 375 ml (1½ cups) vinegar over low heat. Add the jams to the remaining vinegar and stir well, using a wooden spoon. Add the remaining ingredients, including the onion mixture, and stir. Pour the mixture into the warm vinegar and bring to the boil, stirring occasionally. Set aside to cool, then bottle and refrigerate.

Makes about 1¼ litres (5 cups)

Piccalilli (page 92) and Apricot and Peach Chutney

CHAPTER 9

COOKING FOR LARGE NUMBERS

Religious ceremonies, weddings, births and funerals
– these form an important part of the Malay calendar
where family, friends and neighbours feast together, so it's
essential that we know how to cater for large groups.

VEGETABLE MUTTON CURRY

A fairly expensive meal, so save it for when your relatives are visiting on the weekend.

60 ml (¼ cup) oil
3 pieces stick cinnamon
2 large onions, chopped
1 kg thin lamb ribs
500 g mutton knuckles
500 ml (2 cups) water
1 kg lamb leg chops, cubed
10 ml (2 tsp) tomato sauce
1 small tomato, blanched, peeled and pulped
6 thin slices green pepper
1 small spitskop cabbage (curly top), shredded
1 bunch young carrots, peeled and cut into rounds
5 ml (1 tsp) turmeric
5 ml (1 tsp) leaf masala
5 ml (1 tsp) garlic and ginger paste
500 g new potatoes

1 bunch young turnips, peeled and sliced
5 ml (1 tsp) sugar
10 ml (2 tsp) medium-coarse salt
2 starseed petals (star anise)
6 curry leaves
2.5 ml (½ tsp) ground jeera (cumin)

Heat the oil in a large heavy-based saucepan over medium heat. Add the cinnamon and onion, and brown. Stir, then add the ribs and knuckles, and cook for 20 minutes in 375 ml (1½ cups) water. Now add the cubed chops and simmer for another 20 minutes. Braise once, then add the remaining 125 ml (½ cup) water. Add the remaining ingredients, except the jeera. Stir thoroughly and simmer slowly over low heat until almost done. Finally add the jeera.
Serves 14

MUTTON CURRY

A mouth-watering curry with plenty of thick gravy, traditionally served at weddings with rice or roti.

250 ml (1 cup) oil
5 pieces stick cinnamon
6 cardamom pods, slightly cracked
4 large onions, chopped
10 ml (2 tsp) turmeric
10 ml (2 tsp) leaf masala
2 ripe tomatoes, blanched, peeled and pulped
15 ml (1 tbsp) tomato sauce
1 kg lamb hindquarter, cubed
2 kg lamb leg chops, cubed
1 kg shoulder of mutton, cubed
20 ml (1½ tbsp) medium-coarse salt
500 ml (2 cups) water
2 kg small potatoes, peeled and halved
10 cloves garlic, crushed
15 ml (1 tbsp) crushed fresh ginger
1 green pepper, chopped

40 ml (2½ tbsp) gharum masala or jeera (cumin) seeds or powder
2 starseed petals (star anise)
10 ml (2 tsp) fine, dry breadcrumbs
5 ml (1 tsp) sugar
125 ml (½ cup) chopped green dhania (coriander) leaves

Heat the oil, cinnamon and cardamon in a saucepan over medium heat. Add the onion and brown before adding the turmeric, masala, tomato and tomato sauce. Stir well, then add the cubed meat and salt. Cook, covered, for 20 minutes, braising once and stirring thoroughly. Add the water and cook, still covered, until the meat is tender. Now add the potatoes and remaining ingredients with very little water if necessary. Reduce the heat. Stir thoroughly once or twice and simmer until the potatoes are cooked. Serve this meal with Cinnamon Pumpkin (page 78) Lemon and Brinjal Atjar (page 97) and Bulk Rice (page 105) or roti.
Serves 24

Mutton Curry, Lemon and Brinjal Atjar (page 97)
and Malay Roti (page 142)

COOKING FOR LARGE NUMBERS **103**

MASALA AND GARLIC CHICKEN

It's such a delicious meal that you'll be surprised by how easy it is to make.

2 x 1 kg chickens
a few slices red or green pepper
20 ml (1½ tbsp) medium-coarse salt
3 cloves garlic, crushed
30 ml (2 tbsp) red, roasted masala
30 ml (2 tbsp) peri-peri oil
1 kg new potatoes
oil for deep-frying

Rub the chicken skin with red or green pepper. Then salt chicken all over and set aside for a few minutes. Mix garlic, masala and peri-peri oil in a saucer, rub into chicken and marinate for 30 minutes.

Transfer to a roasting pan. Grill on middle shelf for 1 hour at 200°C, basting occasionally with the cooking juices until chicken is tender.

Deep-fry whole potatoes in hot oil and serve alongside chicken with Beetroot and Onion Salad (page 85) and Sweet Sultana Yellow Rice (page 81).

Serves 10

NOTES:
- One small chilli, chopped, or a pinch of cayenne pepper can be added to give the Sosati Curry more bite. Serve with Cinnamon Rice (page 81).
- A pressure cooker will cook your food in half the time of that of an ordinary saucepan.
- Heat the stove plate before placing your pot on it. This will save you cooking time and electricity.
- When bulk cooking, first lightly braise the onions, then add the meat, which must be well drained, otherwise it will shred.
- Chicken dishes should always be cooked on medium heat.

SOSATI CURRY

When catering for a large Sunday party, this is a choice meal to serve.

125 ml (½ cup) boiling water
90 g (¾ cup) tamarind
10 ml (2 tsp) sugar
2 kg lamb cutlets
1 large onion, chopped
10 ml (2 tsp) medium-coarse salt
1 sliced red or green pepper
10 cloves garlic, crushed
6 allspice
4 cardamom pods
2 bay leaves
2 whole cloves
5 ml (1 tsp) turmeric
10 ml (2 tsp) red roasted masala
250 ml (1 cup) cold water
15 ml (1 tbsp) oil
10 ml (2 tsp) fine, dry breadcrumbs

Pour the boiling water over tamarind and sugar, and leave to soak in the water for a few minutes. Drain and set aside. Over medium heat, arrange the cutlets on the base of a saucepan, top with the onion, salt and remaining ingredients, except the tamarind, water, oil and breadcrumbs. Braise until well browned. Add the cold water and oil, cover and cook for 30 minutes. Uncover and allow to brown a little. Reduce the heat, adding extra cold water in very small quantities if necessary. Simmer for a further 30 minutes. Finally add the tamarind pulp and liquid and the breadcrumbs. This is a semi-dry meal, so the sauce should not be too runny. Serve with boiled potatoes and saffron rice. Two drops of egg yellow food colouring can be substituted for the saffron and two pieces stick cinnamon make the rice sweeter.

Serves 18

MINCE AND VEGETABLE BREYANI

The meat, vegetables and rice are served in one pot – a good meal for a large group.

125 ml (½ cup) oil
4 pieces stick cinnamon
1 large onion, chopped
10 ml (2 tsp) tomato sauce
1 small tomato, blanched, peeled and pulped
1 cauliflower, broken into florets
6 carrots, peeled and stubbed
375 ml (1½ cups) water
7.5 ml (1½ tsp) leaf masala
5 ml (1 tsp) turmeric
½ spitskop cabbage (curly top), shredded
10 ml (2 tsp) medium-coarse salt
1.5 kg coarse steak mince
1 x 410 g tin whole kernel corn
10 ml (2 tsp) garlic, crushed
10 ml (2 tsp) ginger paste
500 g frozen green beans
5 ml (1 tsp) gharum masala

RICE
700 g (3½ cups) uncooked long-grain white rice
1 litre (4 cups) boiling water
10 ml (2 tsp) salt
2 pieces stick cinnamon
4 cardamom pods
5 ml (1 tsp) turmeric

Heat the oil and cinnamon together over medium heat. Toss in the onion and brown, then add the tomato sauce and tomato pulp. Stir briefly, then add the cauliflower, carrots and 250 ml (1 cup) cold water. Steam for 10 minutes. Now add the masala, turmeric, cabbage and salt with 125 ml (½ cup) water, and steam for a further 5 minutes. Add the mince and remaining ingredients, except the gharum masala. Stir thoroughly and simmer, uncovered. Water can be added after about 15 minutes if necessary. The saucepan must be almost dry. Stir, remove from the heat and add the beans.

Now cook the rice in boiling water with the salt, cinnamon, cardamom and turmeric. Drain, strain and steam in a colander over rapidly boiling water for 10 minutes. Allow to cool. Mix the breyani mixture and rice together, then sprinkle the gharum masala lightly over the breyani. Cover the saucepan and steam for a further 10 minutes over low heat. Serve with Lemon and Kumquat Atjar (page 98) or Apple Sambal (page 95).
Serves 20

BULK RICE

2 kg uncooked long-grain white rice
4 litres (12 cups) boiling water
100 g (½ cup) medium-coarse salt
2 whole cloves
2 small leeks, finely chopped
30 ml (2 tbsp) oil
2.5 ml (½ tsp) turmeric
30 ml (2 tbsp) butter

Use two saucepans to cook in and divide all the ingredients in half. Cook the rice in the boiling water in the two pans with the remaining ingredients, except the butter, for about 25 minutes or until tender. Drain and fast-steam the rice in colanders with the butter until hot.
Serves 20

LABARANG OVEN FRIKKADELS

An all-time favourite which is often served at weddings and other joyous occasions.

3 kg coarse steak mince
2 loaves stale white bread, sliced, soaked in water for 5 minutes and squeezed dry
500 ml (2 cups) cold water
2 large onions, chopped
4 large eggs
25 ml (1½ tbsp) medium-coarse salt
½ bunch parsley, chopped
20 mint leaves, finely chopped
7.5 ml (1½ tsp) ground nutmeg
15 ml (1 tbsp) ground black pepper
4 green chillies, chopped
½ small red or green pepper, chopped
7.5 ml (1½ tsp) turmeric
10 ml (2 tsp) red masala
250 g (1 cup) soft butter
1 firm tomato, diced

Wash the mince in a colander or sieve under slow-running cold water. Drain well, then combine the mince and bread, and mix well in a large basin. Add the remaining ingredients, except the tomato. Using both hands, work very lightly and slowly, making sure that everything is blended thoroughly. Now add the tomato. Shape into frikkadels or spread the mixture evenly in a large baking sheet and cut into squares when done. Bake on the middle shelf of the oven at 180 °C for 30–40 minutes, depending on the size of the frikkadels or the height of the mixture in the baking sheet. Serve with mashed potato, peas, and Beetroot and Onion Salad (page 85).
Makes 86 frikkadels

LABARANG KABOBS

These oblong frikkadels consist of hard-boiled eggs wrapped in mince and fried – they are usually served at Eidul-Fitr (Labarang).

6 slices stale bread, soaked in water for 5 minutes and squeezed dry
1 kg coarse steak mince
1 onion, chopped
1 tomato, blanched, peeled and pulped
1 egg
60 ml (¼ cup) chopped parsley
2.5 ml (½ tsp) ground nutmeg
7.5 ml (1½ tsp) salt
5 ml (1 tsp) pepper
6 cloves garlic, crushed
136 g (½ cup) butter or margarine
10 hard-boiled eggs, halved lengthwise
oil for frying

Mix all the ingredients together except the hard-boiled eggs and oil. If the mixture is still too stiff, add a little water. Form into ovals and put half a hard-boiled egg into each kebab. Fry in very warm oil until done and serve with yellow rice and salads.
Makes 20

NOTE: The Labarang Kabobs can be oven-fried or lightly pan-fried.

Labarang Kabobs and Sweet Sultana Yellow Rice (page 81)

OLD CAPE DENNINGVLEIS

Denningvleis is meat flavoured with bay leaves and tamarind, vinegar or lemon juice. The word 'denning' originated from the 'Javanese dendeng', the meat of the water buffalo – but nowadays we use mutton!

375 ml (1½ cups) oil
2 kg mutton shoulder
2 kg mutton cutlets
2 kg thick mutton ribs
1 kg onions, chopped
2 whole heads of garlic, crushed
30 ml (2 tbsp) medium-coarse salt
20 ml (1½ tbsp) ground black pepper
10 whole cloves
25 allspice
20 bay leaves
7.5 ml (1½ tsp) ground nutmeg
250 g (1 cup) tamarind
500 ml (2 cups) boiling water
10 ml (2 tsp) sugar
2 large green peppers, chopped
45 ml (3 tbsp) fine, dry breadcrumbs

MASHED POTATO
6 kg small potatoes, peeled and halved
15 ml (1 tbsp) baking powder
1.5 litres (6 cups) milk
5 ml (1 tsp) ground nutmeg

Heat the oil in a large catering saucepan over medium heat. Cut the meat into suitably-sized pieces and spread on the base of the saucepan. Add the onion, spices and remaining ingredients, except the tamarind, boiling water, sugar, peppers and breadcrumbs. Cover the saucepan and braise the meat until tender, adding small amounts of water to the saucepan. Meanwhile soak the tamarind and sugar in boiling water for a few minutes, drain and set aside. When the meat is braised and well browned, add the peppers and tamarind pulp and liquid (remove pips) to the saucepan. Denning stew should not be too saucy. To thicken the sauce, add the breadcrumbs when the cooking is done, 5 minutes before serving. Boil the potatoes until soft, then mash with the baking powder, milk and nutmeg. Serve the stew with mashed potatoes and Glazed Carrots (page 82).
Serves 40

PERI-PERI CHICKEN

The peri-peri oil makes the chicken succulent and adds a lively tang to the dish.

4 medium chickens, cut into portions
30 ml (2 tbsp) medium-coarse salt
15 ml (1 tbsp) red masala
60 ml (¼ cup) peri-peri oil
15 ml (1 tbsp) ground cinnamon
125 g (½ cup) margarine
10 pieces stick cinnamon
250 ml (1 cup) water

Clean the chicken well. Mix the salt, masala, peri-peri oil and ground cinnamon together, rub into the chicken and leave to stand for 1 hour. Melt the margarine over medium heat in a catering saucepan. Add the chicken with the cinnamon sticks and cook quickly until the chicken is browned. Add the water and cook until tender, then grill until the chicken is crisp and golden brown. Serve with potato chips or rice.
Serves 20

SMOKED MUSSEL AND BABY CLAM CURRY

This queen of shellfish dishes can be served as a delicious starter and takes only 20 minutes to prepare.

250 ml (1 cup) boiling water
30 g (2 tbsp) tamarind
10 ml (2 tsp) sugar
125 ml (½ cup) oil
1 large onion, chopped
1 small tomato, blanched, peeled
and pulped
10 ml (2 tsp) tomato sauce
5 ml (1 tsp) turmeric
5 ml (1 tsp) red leaf masala
1 cardamom pod
2 pieces stick cinnamon
375 ml (1½ cups) water
3 x 290 g tin baby clams, drained
1 x 525 g tin smoked mussels in
cottonseed oil

¼ green pepper, chopped
2.5 ml (½ tsp) medium-coarse salt
5 ml (1 tsp) garlic and ginger paste
a pinch jeera (cumin) seeds or
ground jeera
10 curry leaves with stalks

Pour boiling water onto the tamarind, add the sugar, stir and set aside. Heat the oil in a heavy-based saucepan on high heat. Toss in the onion and brown a little. Stir once or twice, then add the tomato pulp and sauce, turmeric, masala, cardamom, cinnamon and water. Reduce the heat to low. Drain the tamarind through a sieve into a saucepan. Gently add the baby clams, mussels and remaining ingredients. Stir to heat through. Serve immediately in small bowls lined with lettuce leaves, cocktail rolls on the side, or serve on a bed of fluffy white rice.

Serves 15 as a starter

Smoked Mussel and Baby Clam Curry

CHAPTER 10

PUDDINGS

Partial to puddings, the traditional Malay favours desserts,
which are usually baked. Lighter, fresher fridge desserts
with fruit as the base are lavishly decorated with cream,
cherries and chocolate vermicelli.

VINEGAR PUDDING

Some people call this malva pudding – it's such a 'lekker' pudding that you won't be able to stop eating until it's finished!

75 g (5 tbsp) soft butter
185 ml (¾ cup) soft brown sugar
2 eggs, beaten
15 ml (1 tbsp) apricot jam
15 ml (1 tbsp) vinegar
375 ml (1½ cups) milk
a pinch salt
4 x 250 ml (4 cups) self-raising flour
2.5 ml (½ tsp) bicarbonate of soda

SAUCE
500 ml (2 cups) boiling water
100 g (½ cup) soft butter
125 ml (½ cup) soft brown sugar
5 ml (1 tsp) treacle (see page 124)
250 ml (1 cup) evaporated milk

Cream the butter, sugar and eggs together, add the remaining ingredients and mix well. Turn into a greased ovenproof dish and bake at 140 °C on the middle shelf for 30 minutes. To make the sauce, combine and heat the ingredients together, stirring until hot. Remove from the heat and pour over the warm pudding. Serve topped with cream and pecan nuts, if desired.
Serves 8-10

SAGO PUDDING

Once the sago has been soaked, this is a regular weekend pud that's quick and easy to prepare!

250 ml (1 cup) sugar
3 large eggs
5 ml (1 tsp) vanilla essence
250 ml (1 cup) sago, soaked in water for 3 hours, then drained
a pinch salt
a pinch ground cinnamon
500 ml (2 cups) milk
a pinch ground nutmeg
90 g (⅓ cup) butter or margarine, sliced
15 ml (1 tbsp) cake flour, made into a thin paste with a little water

Cream the sugar and eggs for 2 minutes, then add the vanilla essence. Stir in the sago and remaining ingredients, except the nutmeg, butter and flour paste, and transfer to a greased ovenproof dish. Stir in the sliced butter and flour paste, and sprinkle with the nutmeg. Preheat the oven to 180 °C and bake the pudding on the middle shelf for about 30 minutes. Serve hot with stewed raisins and honey, or green fig preserve syrup.
Serves 4-6

Vinegar Pudding

BAKED DATE PUDDING

This is my favourite pudding, an olden time dessert learnt from my granny.

90 g (⅓ cup) soft butter
125 ml (½ cup) soft brown sugar
2 large eggs, beaten
250 ml (1 cup) milk
15 ml (1 tbsp) oil
a pinch salt
2.5 ml (½ tsp) ground cinnamon
2.5 ml (½ tsp) ground ginger
2.5 ml (½ tsp) ground mixed spice
4 x 250 ml (4 cups) self-raising flour
2.5 ml (½ tsp) bicarbonate of soda
1 x 250 g packet stoneless dates

Cream the butter, sugar and egg together. Add the milk, oil and salt. Mix the dry ingredients together, except the dates, and add to the egg mixture. Finally roll the dates in a little flour and add, mixing well. Turn out into a greased ovenproof dish. Bake on the middle shelf at 180 °C for 40 minutes and serve with thin custard.

Serves 6–8

APRICOT JAM BAKED PUDDING

You can serve this hot or cold – I prefer to eat it hot.

125 g (½ cup) butter or margarine
250 ml (1 cup) sugar
2 eggs, beaten
10 ml (2 tsp) oil
4 x 250 ml (4 cups) self-raising flour
a pinch salt
250 ml (1 cup) milk
5 ml (1 tsp) treacle (see page 78)
15 ml (1 tbsp) apricot jam
2.5 ml (½ tsp) bicarbonate of soda

Cream the butter and sugar together, then add the eggs. Blend well, then add the oil, flour, salt, milk, treacle and jam. Stir thoroughly, add the bicarbonate of soda and mix well. Pour into a well-greased baking tin or bread tin – it mustn't be too shallow. Bake at 180 °C on the middle shelf for 30 minutes. Serve hot or cold with thin custard.

Serves 6–8

BOEBER

Boeber is a ceremonial drink but we also serve it as a dessert in winter – and sometimes even for breakfast!

15 ml (1 tbsp) butter
3 small cinnamon sticks
2 cardamom pods
250 ml (1 cup) lockshen, slightly crushed
125 ml (½ cup) sago, soaked for 2 hours and drained
500 ml (2 cups) boiling water
60 ml (4 tbsp) condensed milk
a pinch salt

Heat the butter in a saucepan over medium heat. When soft, stir in the cinnamon, cardamom and lockshen, and cook until the lockshen is light brown. Now add the sago, stir to mix, then add the remaining ingredients. Cook for about 15 minutes, stirring occasionally. If left to stand, the boeber will thicken. Before serving in individual glasses or bowls, add a little milk to each portion.

Serves 4–6

NOTE: Chopped almonds or seedless sultanas can be added to the Boeber if desired.

LOCKSHEN DELIGHT

Lockshen is similar to vermicelli but thinner. You'll find it in supermarkets in the pasta section.

180 g (¾ cup) butter or margarine
2 x 250 g boxes lockshen
200 g (1 cup) white sugar
750 ml (3 cups) water
100 g (¾ cup) pecan or Brazil nuts, chipped, or sultanas/ seedless raisins

Melt the butter in a saucepan over medium heat, add the lockshen and stir continuously and vigorously until golden brown. Add the sugar and water, and cover the saucepan. Reduce the heat to very low and simmer for 10 minutes. Stir the lockshen lightly to ensure that it doesn't dry out – if it does, add a little warm water. Serve hot or cold in small bowls, decorated with nuts, sultanas or raisins.
Serves 12

Lockshen Delight

STRAWBERRY FRIDGE DESSERT

250 g fresh strawberries,
washed and hulled
30 ml (2 tbsp) white sugar
40 ml (2½ tbsp) cold water
1 extra-large egg, separated
10 ml (2 tsp) custard powder
750 ml (3 cups) hot water
2.5 ml (½ tsp) gelatine
2 x 80 g packets strawberry jelly
chocolate vermicelli for decoration

Cut the strawberries into uneven pieces and place in a small saucepan. Add the sugar and 30 ml (2 tbsp) cold water, then simmer for 10 minutes. Meanwhile, combine the egg yolk, custard powder and 10 ml (2 tsp) cold water. Stir well and add to the strawberry mixture, stirring rapidly for a few minutes. Remove from the heat and set aside to cool. Allow the hot water to cool a little, then stir in the gelatine and jelly. Leave to cool. When cold, add the strawberry mixture and blend thoroughly. Beat the egg white until frothy and fold in. Pour into a glass dish. Top with the chocolate vermicelli, chill and serve. Sliced strawberries and cream make a good topping too.
SERVES 8–10

PEAR SNOW

Light and delicious, perfect for rounding off a hot, spicy meal.

7.5 ml (1½ tsp) gelatine
2 x 80 g packets lemon jelly
500 ml (2 cups) hot water
1 x 825 g tin pears, drained and
syrup reserved
1 x 410 g tin evaporated milk,
chilled overnight
50 g Peppermint Crisp, chipped
10 pecan nuts, slightly crushed

In a large bowl, combine 5 ml (1 tsp) gelatine with the jelly, slowly adding the hot water. Stir well and set aside. Mash the pears and set aside. Heat the pear syrup over low heat with the remaining gelatine. Stir, then remove from the heat and add to the jelly. In a deep mixing bowl, whisk or beat the evaporated milk vigorously until very stiff, add to the pear mixture and then add the jelly. Stir slowly until well blended. Pour into a glass bowl, decorate with the chipped chocolate and top with the nuts.
Serves 8

TAMELETJIES

Pine kernels are very expensive – why not collect the ones that have fallen from the pine trees, like we used to? Coarse coconut dyed with the food colouring of your choice can be used instead of the kernels.

500 ml (2 cups) caramel sugar
5 ml (1 tsp) honey
375 ml (1½ cups) boiling water
100 g (¾ cup) pine kernels
2.5 ml (½ tsp) cream of tartar

Before you begin, make 3 large or 6 small rectangular containers out of aluminium foil or greaseproof paper, 2 cm high x 6 cm wide x 12 cm long. In the old days, lined pages from exercise books were used. The four corners will stay together because of the stickiness of the tameletjie. Add the sugar and honey to the boiling water; bring to the boil again. Cook on low heat until the sugar begins to bubble. Stir for about 2 minutes or until the syrup starts to get sticky. Remove from the heat and allow to cool. Stir in the pine kernels, then add the cream of tartar and mix well. Spoon the mixture into the containers (or any shallow container) so they are three-quarters full. Leave in the fridge to set for 1 hour.
Makes 3 large or 6 small containers

SUMMER PEAR FLAN

You'll need special flan baking tins for this recipe.

45 ml (3 tbsp) milk
45 ml (3 tbsp) water
120 g (½ cup) butter
250 ml (1 cup) castor sugar
2 eggs, separated, whites
lightly beaten
500 ml (2 cups) cake flour
10 ml (2 tsp) baking powder
1 x 410 g tin pears in thick syrup,
drained and syrup reserved
a pinch gelatine

Place the milk, water and butter in a saucepan, and bring to the boil, stirring gently. Remove from the heat and set aside to cool. When completely cool, add the sugar and beat well. Now add the egg yolks, then fold in the egg whites and finally the flour and baking powder. Pour the mixture into two flan baking tins that have been wiped with a few grains of salt before greasing. Bake at 180 °C for 25–30 minutes. Set aside to cool completely and turn out onto a plate when cold. Heat the pear syrup, combined with the gelatine, over low heat. Stir until almost boiling. Remove from the heat and cool completely. Chill a little in the fridge and remove the moment it starts to set. Pour over the flan cases and decorate with the pears. Serve chilled.
Serves 6

NOTES:
- The pears can be replaced with tinned apricots, peaches, pineapple or other fruit, if preferred.
- To prevent possible mouth sores from pineapple, rub pineapple lightly with salt after peeling.
- A few drops of lemon juice added to the water before apples are placed in the pot will prevent discolouring.
- Always sift flour before using it.

JAM TART

8 x 250 ml (8 cups) cake flour
750 g (3 cups) butter, chilled
5 ml (1 tsp) salt
2 eggs, separated, yolks beaten
750 ml (3 cups) iced water
10 ml (2 tsp) cream of tartar
60 ml (¼ cup) cornflour
1 x 450 g tin apricot whole fruit jam
15 ml (1 tbsp) lemon juice
2 eggs, beaten with
10 ml (2 tsp) milk

Set aside 60 ml (¼ cup) flour for rolling out the dough. Sift the remaining flour and coarsely grate 250 g (1 cup) butter. Mix the flour, butter, salt and egg yolks. Make a soft, firm dough by gradually adding the water. Roll out the dough and spread thin slices of butter over. Add the cream of tartar to the cornflour. Top the dough with a few sprinkles of this mix. Fold the dough unevenly and roll out with a little flour rubbed onto the rolling pin. Repeat the process until all the butter has been used. Cut the pastry into two or three manageable pieces. Chill in the fridge overnight. Roll out the pastry and line tart plates. Spread three-quarters of the jam over the pastry. Bake on the middle shelf for 12–15 minutes at 200 °C. When the tarts are done, gloss with the beaten egg. Cover with a cloth for a few minutes before removing from the tins.
Makes 4 large tarts

POTATO PUDDING

Delicious cut into squares and decorated with stewed fruit.

500 g small potatoes, peeled
and halved
6 eggs, beaten
125 g (½ cup) butter
250 ml (1 cup) sugar
5 ml (1 tsp) salt
2 drops almond essence
5 ml (1 tsp) vanilla essence
2.5 ml (½ tsp) ground cinnamon
1 litre (4 cups) milk
15 ml (1 tbsp) cake flour, made into a
paste with 60 ml (¼ cup) milk

Boil, drain and mash the potatoes. Mix all the ingredients together, except the milk and flour paste, using half the butter. Now add the milk, flour paste and remaining butter. Bake in a greased ovenproof dish at 180 °C on the middle shelf for about 40 minutes.

Serves 10–12

PINEAPPLE FRIDGE DESSERT

Minneolas or apples can be substituted for the pineapple – remember to use the appropriate flavour jelly and essence for the different fruits.

1 large queen pineapple, grated
15 ml (1 tbsp) white sugar
45 ml (3 tbsp) cold water
10 ml (2 tsp) custard powder
2 eggs, separated
2.5 ml (½ tsp) gelatine
750 ml (3 cups) hot water
2 x 80 g packets pineapple jelly
a drop pineapple essence

Cook the pineapple and sugar in 30 ml (2 tbsp) water in a saucepan over medium heat for 10 minutes, stirring occasionally. In the meantime, add 15 ml (1 tbsp) cold water to the custard powder and egg yolks, and mix well. Pour the custard mixture into a saucepan, stirring vigorously. Remove from the heat and leave to cool. Add the gelatine and hot water to the jelly powder, stir, then add the essence. Beat the egg whites until stiff. When everything has cooled, gently fold the fruit mixture and egg whites into the jelly. Mix thoroughly. Transfer to the freezer for 30 minutes. Remove to the fridge, top with well-beaten fresh cream and decorate with chopped nuts and cherries before serving.

Serves 8–10

Pineapple Fridge Dessert

CHAPTER 11

CAKES, TARTS AND BISCUITS

Biscuit and cake tins are always full in case of unexpected visitors. Here I've given some of our traditional recipes, as well as some which have been adopted by our community.

CAFE  ☾★ 1 HUNDRED

KAROO KAROO

100

Rose Corner CAFE

100

ROSE CORNER C...
FULL CREAM
MILK
100% PURE
FARM FRESH TASTE

Special

SMOKE FISH (vis) TO-DAY

HOT KOEKSISTERS
SUNDAYS

PIES
STEAK & KIDNEY
PEPPER STEAK
STEAK
CHIC. & MUSHROOM

OROS
READY TO DRINK

Fresh
HOT
PIES &
SAMOOSAS
Daily

PUFF PASTRY

15 ml (1 tbsp) cornflour
2.5 ml (½ tsp) cream of tartar
4 x 250 ml (4 cups) cake flour
375 g (1½ cups) butter, chilled
30 ml (2 tbsp) oil
juice of ½ lemon
1 egg yolk, beaten
250 ml (1 cup) iced water

Mix the cornflour and cream of tartar; set aside. Sift the flour and rub in 60 g (¼ cup) of butter. Add the rest of the ingredients, except the remaining butter, to make a pastry. Roll out the pastry on a floured surface and flake pieces of butter unevenly over it. Dredge the cornflour and cream of tartar mixture over; fold the pastry unevenly. Roll out twice more until all the butter has been used; chill for a few hours.
Makes 3 large tart shells

ZAINAB'S APPLE TART

This easy, mouth-watering recipe is guaranteed to satisfy the hungriest of friends! Make the pastry as per the instructions for the Milk Tart on page 127.

FILLING
5 cooking apples, peeled, cored and thickly wedged
1 clove
10 ml (2 tsp) golden syrup (optional)
a pinch ground cinnamon
15 ml (1 tbsp) soft brown sugar
60 ml (¼ cup) water
handful seedless raisins (optional)

Simmer the apples, clove, golden syrup, if using, cinnamon, sugar and water until soft and brown. The mixture must be syrupy rather than liquid. Set aside to cool. Roll out the pastry on a floured surface and line a greased pie dish with it, keeping a little of the pastry aside for the topping. Spread the apple mixture onto the pastry, scatter over the raisins, if using, and grate or crumble the remaining pastry over. Bake at 180 °C for 30 minutes or until golden brown.
Serves 8

KOLWYNTJIES

Kolwyntjies are also known as queen cakes.

125 g (½ cup) butter
250 ml (1 cup) castor sugar
3 eggs, beaten
125 ml (½ cup) orange juice
5 ml (1 tsp) grated orange rind
4 x 250 ml (4 cups) self-raising flour
5 ml (1 tsp) baking powder
125 ml (½ cup) currants
60 ml (¼ cup) oil

Cream the butter and sugar together well, then add the eggs. Now add the remaining ingredients and stir thoroughly, adding a little milk if the mixture is too dry. Preheat the oven to 180 °C and bake in greased patty pans or paper cups for 10 minutes, or until they are golden brown.
Makes about 50

Opposite: Zainab's Apple Tart

TREACLE

Treacle gives any chocolate cake, dark cake or pudding a good colour and flavour.

625 ml (2½ cups) yellow sugar
about 250 ml (1 cup) water

Heat a heavy-based pot on medium heat and add the sugar, allowing it to burn. Do not stir. When the sugar has melted completely, add a cup of water and stir until the sugar has changed colour to very dark brown. Remove from the heat and, when cold, bottle in a wide-necked jar, seal well and store for further use. The treacle should be liquid enough to pour.
Makes about 500 ml

ANISEED DOUGHNUTS

You can make these oval doughnuts the day before and the syrup just before serving.

15 g (1 tbsp) instant dry yeast
60 ml (¼ cup) self-raising flour
750 ml (3 cups) cake flour
100 g (½ cup) butter
2 eggs, beaten
30 ml (2 tbsp) sugar
5 ml (1 tsp) aniseed
5 ml (1 tsp) salt
375 ml (1½ cups) milk
375 ml (1½ cups) oil

SYRUP
250 ml (1 cup) white sugar
10 ml (2 tsp) honey or golden syrup
250 ml (1 cup) warm water

Mix the yeast with a pinch of sugar and 10 ml (2 tsp) warm water, and allow to stand for a few seconds until it froths. Sift the flours lightly, then rub in the butter. Add the remaining ingredients, except the oil, to form a dough, but do not knead. Cover with plastic wrap or a cloth, and leave in a warm place for 1½–2 hours or until doubled in size, then turn out onto a floured surface. Dip the fingers into the flour and stretch the dough. Work with light movements and form into ovals. Heat the oil in a deep saucepan and fry the doughnuts over medium heat for a few minutes until they have cracked slightly and are golden brown. To make the syrup, add the sugar and honey or golden syrup to the warm water. Allow to boil until the sugar has melted, then leave to cool completely. Prick each doughnut with a fork and, using a slotted spoon, sweep through the syrup, drain and transfer to a platter.
Makes about 25

Opposite: Koeksisters

KOEKSISTERS

These oblong koeksisters are often served in Malay homes on Sunday mornings. They can be deep-fried and frozen (without the syrup) for up to 14 days. Thaw for 1 hour, make the syrup and enjoy!

250 ml (1 cup) cake flour
250 ml (1 cup) self-raising flour
5 ml (1 tsp) salt
60 g (¼ cup) butter
5 ml (1 tsp) ground ginger
5 ml (1 tsp) ground cinnamon
5 ml (1 tsp) ground mixed spice
2.5 ml (½ tsp) ground cardamom
10 ml (2 tsp) soft brown sugar
10 ml (2 tsp) white sugar
7.5 ml (1½ tsp) instant dry yeast
375 ml (1½ cups) warm water

SYRUP
250 ml (1 cup) water
125 ml (½ cup) sugar
15 ml (1 tbsp) desiccated coconut
1 piece of naartjie peel

In a mixing bowl, combine the flours with the salt. Add the butter and rub in lightly until it resembles fine breadcrumbs. Add the remaining ingredients, using the warm water to form a dough. Do not knead. Cover with plastic and leave in a warm place for about 1½ –2 hours or until doubled in size, then turn out onto a lightly floured surface. Dip the fingers and knife into flour and use your hands to stretch the dough. Cut into 4 x 8 cm strips and deep-fry over medium heat in a deep saucepan. Insert a fork to check if done and remove quickly, one by one. Drain in a colander or on kitchen paper. To make the syrup, bring the water, sugar, coconut and naartjie peel to a slow boil in a large saucepan until the syrup starts to bubble. Prick each koeksister, then lower into the syrup. Add as many koeksisters to the syrup as the pan will hold. Turn the koeksisters and cook for 5 minutes each side or until browned. Remove from the pan with a slotted spoon, placing them on a platter sprinkled with a little extra coconut. Sprinkle coconut over each layer of koeksisters and serve while hot with choice coffee.

Makes about 25

NOTES:
- The best place to leave dough to rise is in a warm bed! Place the covered dough in a mixing bowl on layers of newspaper on top of the blankets.
- Dried naartjie peel lasts indefinitely when stored in a jar. Dry it in the sun or in the oven at a temperature below 100 °C. Add naartjie peel to koeksisters, doughnuts, sweet potatoes or stewed mealies.

JAM ROLL

A firm favourite in our community.

5 eggs, separated
250 ml (1 cup) castor sugar
5 ml (1 tsp) vanilla essence
a pinch of fine salt
250 ml (1 cup) self-raising flour
10 ml (2 tsp) baking powder

FILLING
45 ml (3 tbsp) jam of your choice

Beat the egg whites until slightly stiff and set aside. Beat the yolks with the sugar until creamy, then fold in the whites and essence. Add the dry ingredients and blend well to form a batter. Spread the dough on a greased swiss roll tin and bake at 200 °C for 10 minutes. Turn out onto greaseproof paper sprinkled with castor sugar and carefully spread with jam. Quickly roll the cake up inside the greaseproof paper and let it soften for about 30 minutes. Remove the greaseproof paper, cover with a cloth for a few minutes to sweat and cut into slices.
Makes 1 loaf

DATE AND WALNUT LOAF

A favourite childhood recipe.

4 x 250 ml (4 cups) self-raising flour
500 ml (2 cups) cake flour
125 ml (½ cup) white sugar
125 ml (½ cup) soft brown sugar
15 ml (1 tbsp) oil
6 eggs
2.5 ml (½ tsp) vanilla essence
2 x 250 g packets dates rolled in
10 ml (2 tsp) flour
a pinch of salt
500 ml (2 cups) walnuts
300 ml (1¼ cups) yellow sugar
15 ml (1 tbsp) water

Combine all the ingredients, except the yellow sugar and water, and set aside. Place the yellow sugar in a dry pot on low heat and scorch until it is burnt. Remove from the heat, add the water, cover the pot and leave to cool. Add to the rest of the ingredients and bake in a greased loaf tin at 140 °C for 1 hour.
Makes 1 large loaf

CRUMBLED TART

Also called a German tart – serve on special occasions.

PASTRY
250 ml (1 cup) castor sugar
250 g (1 cup) butter
2 large or 3 medium eggs
15 ml (1 tbsp) oil
500 ml (2 cups) cake flour
500 ml (2 cups) self-raising flour

FILLING
625 ml (2½ cups) desiccated coconut
250 ml (1 cup) sugar
125 g (½ cup) apricot jam or
jam of your choice

To make the pastry, cream the sugar and butter together, then add the eggs, oil and flours to form a soft dough. Roll out and press into a greased baking sheet, leaving a little aside for grating over the top. To make the filling, boil the coconut and sugar until almost dry. Spread the jam over the pastry in the baking sheet and cover with the coconut mixture. Grate the remaining pastry over and bake at 180 °C for about 30 minutes until light brown. Cool and cut into squares.
Makes about 10 squares

MILK TART

Serve this with tea and you won't need a meal!

PASTRY
125 g (½ cup) butter
250 ml (¾ cup) castor sugar
5 ml (1 tsp) vanilla essence
1 egg, beaten
250 ml (1 cup) cake flour
250 ml (1 cup) self-raising flour
10 ml (2 tsp) oil
a pinch of salt

FILLING
1 litre (4 cups) milk
10 large eggs
310 ml (1¼ cups) sugar
15 ml (1 tbsp) cake flour, made into
a paste with 30 ml (2 tbsp) water
2.5 ml (½ tsp) ground cardamom

To make the pastry, cream the butter and sugar together, then add the vanilla essence. Add the egg, then gradually add the flours, oil and salt, and work lightly to form a soft and pliable dough. Set aside. To make the filling, slowly bring the milk to the boil. Meanwhile, beat the eggs and sugar together. Remove milk from heat and pour slowly into egg and sugar mixture. Continue stirring, then add the flour paste and set aside. Grease a heavy-based ovenproof dish lightly with butter. Roll out the pastry on a floured surface and line a dish with it. Pour in the filling, place small nuts of butter on top, sprinkle with the ground cardamom and bake on the bottom shelf of the oven at 200°C for 40 minutes.
Serves 10

Milk Tart

CARDAMOM SANDWICH CAKE

125 g (½ cup) soft butter
375 ml (1½ cups) castor sugar
3 eggs, separated
7.5 ml (1½ tsp) ground cardamom
4 x 250 ml (4 cups) self-raising flour
a pinch of salt
5 ml (1 tsp) baking powder
250 ml (½ cup) milk or water
60 ml (¼ cup) oil

Cream the butter and sugar together until smooth, then add the egg yolks and cardamom, stirring in one direction only to prevent holes forming in the mixture. Now the add flour, salt, baking powder and milk or water. Beat the egg whites until stiff and fold in, then add the oil, mixing well. Pour into a greased bread pan and bake at 180 °C on the middle shelf for 1 hour. Remove from the oven and leave to cool in the tins before removing to a wire rack. Cover with a cloth and allow to sweat for about 5 minutes.
Makes 1 loaf

ORANGE LAYER CAKE

Simply delicious served with a cup of tea. Instead of using icing to sandwich the cakes together, use apricot jam.

125 g (½ cup) soft butter
185 ml (¾ cup) castor sugar
a pinch of salt
3 large eggs, separated
juice of 1 large orange
2 drops orange essence
15 ml (1 tbsp) oil
10 ml (2 tsp) grated orange rind
125 ml (½ cup) milk
750 ml (3 cups) cake flour
15 ml (1 tbsp) baking powder

ICING
345 ml (1⅓ cup) icing sugar
60 ml (¼ cup) orange juice
30 ml (2 tbsp) melted butter
60 ml (¼ cup) boiling water

Cream the butter, sugar and salt together. Add the egg yolks, orange juice, essence, oil, rind and milk, mixing well. Beat the egg whites until stiff and fold into the batter. Blend well, then add the flour and baking powder, stirring in one direction only. Grease two round baking tins with oil. Sprinkle 5 ml (1 tsp) flour into each tin and pour equal amounts of batter into each tin. Bake at 180 °C on the middle shelf for 20–25 minutes. Remove from the oven and allow to sweat first by covering with a cloth. When quite cold, remove from the tins. To make the icing, mix all the ingredients together ensuring that the icing is not too runny. Fill and ice the cake by dipping a flat knife or palette knife in cold water to spread the icing more easily, shaking off excess water from the knife. Decorate as desired.
Makes 1 cake

PINEAPPLE TART

Use the Puff Pastry recipe on page 122 to make the base for this tasty tart.

FILLING
1 pineapple, peeled and coarsely grated
60 ml (¼ cup) sugar
250 ml (1 cup) water
1 piece stick cinnamon

TOPPING
60 ml (¼ cup) desiccated coconut
30 ml (2 tbsp) sugar

Make the pastry according to the recipe on page 122. To make the filling, cook the pineapple, sugar, water and cinnamon for 15 minutes over low heat until almost dry. If the pineapple is watery, cook for a little longer. Set aside to cool. To make the topping, cook the coconut and sugar together for about 15 minutes until semi-dry. When everything has cooled completely, roll out the pastry and line tart plates or ordinary porcelain plates, saving some for decorating. Spread the filling into the tart shells, add the topping, cut the remaining pastry into strips and make a criss-cross pattern over the topping. Bake at 200 °C for 5 minutes on the bottom shelf, then transfer to the middle shelf and bake for a further 15 minutes.
Makes 2 tarts

RICH CHOCOLATE CAKE

A bitter-sweet wonder cake!

1 x 125 g tin cocoa
30 ml (2 tbsp) sugar
60 ml (¼ cup) milk
60 ml (¼ cup) water
3 large eggs, separated
125 g (½ cup) soft butter
375 ml (1½ cups) castor sugar
a pinch of salt
750 ml (3 cups) cake flour
15 ml (1 tbsp) baking powder
10 ml (2 tsp) treacle (see page 124)
15 ml (1 tbsp) oil

ICING
60 ml (¼ cup) warm water
240 g (1¾ cups) icing sugar
80 g (⅓ cup) butter

Over low heat, cook a little more than half the tin of cocoa with the sugar, milk and water. Stir to prevent the mixture from sticking to the bottom of the saucepan. Drops of cold water can be added if it is too sticky. Set aside to cool. Beat the egg whites until stiff and set aside. Cream the butter and castor sugar with the salt until smooth. Add the egg yolks, blending well. Stir into the cold chocolate mixture. Sift the flour and baking powder, and stir into the mixture – do not beat, but blend well. Fold in the egg whites, add the treacle and oil, and mix thoroughly. Pour the cake batter into two greased round layer cake tins. Bake at 180 °C for 20 minutes. Remove from the oven. Loosen the cakes with a thin-blade knife and leave in the tins to sweat under a cloth for a few minutes. Turn out onto a wire rack and cover with a dry cloth to prevent drying out. To make the icing, add small amounts of the warm water to the icing sugar, about 60 ml (¼ cup) cocoa (use more cocoa for a more bitter icing) and the butter. Ice the cakes and decorate, if desired, with chocolate twirls or coconut.

Makes 1 cake

Notes:
- Apricot jam can be used to sandwich layer cakes together instead of icing. Or use any jam of your choice.
- Place a lemon in the cake tin and the cake will not dry out while storing.
- It is better to use butter instead of margarine when baking sponge cakes.

Rich Chocolate Cake

FLAN TARTS

Use flan baking tins for these tarts.

FLAN
45 ml (3 tbsp) water
45 ml (3 tbsp) milk
125 g (½ cup) butter
250 ml (1 cup) sugar
3 eggs
4 x 250 ml (4 cups) flour
10 ml (2 tsp) baking powder

FILLING
1 pineapple, peeled and grated
15 ml (1 tbsp) sugar
15 ml (1 tbsp) custard powder

5 ml (1 tsp) butter, melted
1 egg yolk
a little milk
cherry halves for decoration

To make the flans, boil together the water, milk and butter. Allow to cool. Add the sugar and beat. Add the remaining ingredients to form a cake batter. Bake at 180 °C in two flan baking tins for 20–25 minutes. To make the filling, boil the pineapple with the sugar. Make a paste with the custard, butter, egg yolk and a little milk. Stir into the pineapple mixture and boil for 3 minutes. Allow to cool before pouring into flan cases. Decorate with the cherry halves.
Makes 2 flans

CREAM CRACKER TART

My famous Sunday family tart!

CRUST
250 ml (1 cup) cream crackers, crumbled
30 ml (2 tbsp) melted butter
30 ml (2 tbsp) sugar
a pinch ground cinnamon

FILLING
30 ml (2 tbsp) cornflour
2 eggs, separated

250 ml (1 cup) milk
finely ground cinnamon for decoration

Mix the crumbs, butter, sugar and cinnamon together to form a crust. Press into the base of a greased ovenproof pie dish. To make the filling, blend the cornflour and egg yolks with the milk to form a custard. Bring to the boil until thickened. Cool and pour into the crust in pie dish. Whip the egg whites until stiff and spread over the custard. Bake at 180 °C for 30 minutes. Sprinkle with ground cinnamon after baking.
Makes 1 tart

COFFEE LOAF

A tea time loaf, delicious with cheese.

200 g (1⅓ cups) seedless raisins
80 ml (⅓ cup) soft brown sugar
560 ml (2¼ cups) hot, strong liquid coffee
4 x 250 ml (4 cups) self-raising flour
2.5 ml (¼ tsp) ground ginger
60 ml (¼ cup) oil
2.5 ml (½ tsp) salt
5 ml (1 tsp) aniseed
1 egg, beaten
30 ml (2 tbsp) butter, melted

Preheat the oven to 180 °C. Soak the raisins and sugar in the hot coffee for 5 minutes and allow to cool. Sift the flour into a mixing bowl, add the remaining ingredients, including the raisins and sugar, stirring with a wooden spoon. Bake in a well-greased loaf tin for 30–40 minutes. Place on a wire rack, cover with a cloth and leave to sweat for a few minutes before serving.
Makes 1 loaf

NOTES:
- When baking biscuits or pastry, first bake on the second shelf of the oven for 5 minutes, then transfer to the middle shelf for further baking.
- A few drops of lemon juice added to icing gives it a good flavour and colouring.

CORN FLAKE BISCUITS

These ingredients will be in your pantry.

125 g (½ cup) soft butter
125 ml (½ cup) soft brown sugar
2 eggs, beaten
4 x 250 ml (4 cups) corn flakes
2.5 ml (½ tsp) salt
10 ml (2 tsp) oil
375 ml (1½ cups) self-raising flour
2.5 ml (½ tsp) vanilla essence
6 dates, chopped
10 walnuts, quartered

Cream the butter and sugar together. Add the eggs, then the remaining ingredients, working together by hand. Roll out the dough, but not too thinly. Cut out shapes with a cookie cutter and place on a greased baking sheet. Bake at 180 °C on the bottom shelf of the oven for 7 minutes, then on the middle shelf for 10 minutes. Cool on a wire rack.

Makes 36

SABOERATJIES

These traditional biscuits are always decorated with three currants.

4 x 250 ml (4 cups) cake flour
5 ml (1 tsp) baking powder
2 eggs, beaten
200 ml (1 cup) caramel or
soft brown sugar
250 g (1 cup) butter
12 cardamom pods, pounded
5 ml (1 tsp) ground ginger
5 ml (1 tsp) mixed spice
125 ml (½ cup) oil
125 ml (½ cup) currants

Combine all the ingredients, except the currants, to form a dough. Roll out the dough. Cut out with an oblong cookie cutter and place on a greased baking tray. Press three currants in a row down the centre of each cookie. Bake at 180 °C on the second shelf of the oven for 5 minutes, then on the middle shelf for 7 minutes until brown.

Makes about 40

CRUNCHY OAT AND NUT BISCUITS

Dates are often used in Malay cooking – I'm especially fond of baking with them.

125 g (½ cup) butter
250 ml (1 cup) brown sugar
2 eggs, beaten
60 ml (¼ cup) oil
375 ml (1½ cups) self-raising flour
60 g (¼ cup) fine oats
750 ml (3 cups) corn flakes
2 Weet-Bix, crushed
2.5 ml (½ tsp) caramel essence
20 pecan nuts, quartered
½ x 250 g packet dates, chopped
10 ml (2 tsp) ground ginger

Cream the butter and sugar together. Add the eggs, then the remaining ingredients. Mix well and form into balls the size of a large marble. Place on a greased baking tray and flatten slightly with a fork. Bake at 180 °C on the second shelf of the oven for 6 minutes, then on the middle shelf for a further 10 minutes.

Makes about 60

PRONUTRO AND WHOLEMEAL BISCUITS

250 ml (1 cup) wholemeal flour
200 g (1 cup) brown sugar
125 ml (½ cup) wheat germ
250 ml (1 cup) Pronutro
125 ml (½ cup) desiccated coconut
125 g (½ cup) soft butter
a pinch of salt
2 eggs, beaten
15 ml (1 tbsp) oil

Mix the dry ingredients together, then add the remaining ingredients and blend well to form a dough. Roll out the dough on a floured surface and cut into thin sausage shapes about 1½ cm in width and 5 cm long. Place on a greased baking tray and press lightly with a fork. Bake at 180 °C on the middle shelf for 12 minutes.
Makes about 60

SOETKOEKIES

Red bole is available in powder form from pharmacies.

75 g (5 tbsp) butter
75 ml (5 tbsp) oil
400 ml (1½ cups) yellow sugar
5 ml (1 tsp) mixed spice
2.5 ml (½ tsp) ground nutmeg
5 ml (1 tsp) ground cinnamon
2.5 ml (½ tsp) ground cardamom
3 whole cloves, pounded
2 eggs, beaten
4 x 250 ml (4 cups) cake flour
2.5 ml (½ tsp) bicarbonate of soda
5 ml (1 tsp) red bole

Cream the butter, oil and sugar together until soft. Stir in the spices and eggs, mixing well. Sift the flour and bicarbonate of soda together and add, stirring in a little milk if the dough is too dry. Mix the red bole with a third of the dough. Roll out the remaining two-thirds on a floured surface and dot with pieces of the red bole dough. Roll out to ½ cm thick and cut out heart-shaped biscuits with a cutter. Press half a peanut in the centre of each biscuit if desired. Place on a greased baking tray and bake at 200 °C for 5 minutes on the bottom shelf and for a further 10 minutes on the middle shelf.
Makes 50–60

KARAMONK SCRAPS

This is an old recipe for cardamom biscuits, a Malay speciality. If desired, press a tiny pink scented sweet in the middle of each biscuit before baking.

2 eggs
470 ml (2 cups) sugar
125 g (½ cup) butter
4 x 250 ml (4 cups) cake flour
15 ml (1 tbsp) oil
5 ml (1 tsp) baking powder
2.5 ml (½ tsp) rose water
3 cardamom pods, pounded or
5 ml (1 tsp) ground cardamom

Cream the eggs and sugar together well and set aside. Rub the butter into the flour and then lightly mix in the remaining ingredients, including the egg and sugar mixture, to form a soft dough. Roll out to 1 cm thickness. Using cookie cutters, cut into shapes and bake at 180 °C, first on the bottom shelf for 6 minutes and then on the top shelf for a further 6 minutes. Enjoy when cool.
Makes about 60

NOTE: Pound cardamom pods with a hammer between two pieces of greaseproof paper.

GINGER NUTS

These should be slightly sticky when baked.

115 g (½ cup) butter
145 ml (½ cup) soft brown sugar
10 ml (2 tsp) golden syrup
juice of ½ lemon or
15 ml (1 tsp) bottled lemon juice
250 ml (1 cup) cake flour
2.5 ml (½ tsp) baking powder
10 ml (2 tsp) ground ginger

Melt the butter and sugar in a saucepan with the syrup and lemon juice, stirring slowly. Remove from the heat and add the flour, baking powder and ginger. Mix well to form a dough. Place teaspoonfuls of dough on a baking tray lined with well-greased paper. Bake at 200 °C for 10–12 minutes.
Makes about 20

BUTTER BISCUITS

250 g (1 cup) soft butter
7.5 ml (1½ tsp) oil
500 ml (2 cups) yellow sugar
2.5 ml (½ tsp) vanilla essence
1 large egg, beaten
4 x 250 ml (4 cups) cake flour
2.5 ml (½ tsp) bicarbonate of soda

Cream the butter, oil and sugar together until light, then add the essence and egg. Add the flour and bicarbonate of soda, and mix together to form a fairly stiff dough. Roll out the dough on a floured surface and cut out diamond shapes with a cookie cutter. Decorate with pieces of angelica and cherry. Place on a greased baking tray and bake at 200 °C for 10 minutes. Cool on wire racks.
Makes 50

Butter Biscuits, Karamonk Scraps, Saboeratjies (page 131) and Crunchy Oat and Nut Biscuits (page 131)

CHAPTER 12

BREADS AND FRITTERS

Many of these bread recipes are my own creations, tried and tested over the years. I've also included recipes for rotis and pizza dough here. Fritters, with a variety of fillings, are also called 'Vetkoekies' and are often served after dinner.

NUTTY WHEAT BROWN BREAD

The queen of brown breads and simple too.

125 ml (½ cup) wheat germ
60 ml (¼ cup) digestive bran
4 x 250 ml (4 cups) Nutty Wheat Flour
5 ml (1 tsp) medium-coarse salt
2.5 ml (½ tsp) bicarbonate of soda
30 ml (2 tbsp) honey or golden syrup
500 ml (2 cups) stirred Bulgarian yoghurt or buttermilk
250 ml (1 cup) sesame seeds
1 egg, beaten
15 ml (1 tbsp) oil
125 ml (½ cup) milk
7.5 ml (1½ tsp) salt

Preheat the oven to 180°C. Mix all the ingredients together to form a dough. Place the dough in a well-greased baking tin and bake on the middle shelf for about 1 hour and 10 minutes. Use a skewer to test if the bread is ready – if the skewer comes out clean, the bread is ready. Place on a wire rack to cool, cover with a cloth and leave to sweat for a few minutes.

Makes 1 loaf

SPECIAL MILK LOAVES

8 x 250 ml (8 cups) cake flour
500 ml (2 cups) self-raising flour
500 ml (2 cups) milk
250 ml (1 cup) water
30 ml (2 tbsp) sugar
7.5 ml (1½ tsp) salt
15 g (1 tbsp) instant dry yeast
2 eggs, beaten

Sift the flours in a mixing bowl. Heat the milk and water together until warm but not too hot, remove from the stove and add the sugar, salt and yeast. Pour most of the milk mixture into the flour and knead to form a dough. Add the beaten eggs and the rest of the milk mixture, working the dough with your hands for 5 minutes. Cover the dough completely with plastic and leave to rise for about 2 hours. Turn out onto a floured surface and cut into 3 pieces. Working lightly, punch down and place in three greased baking tins to prove for 30 minutes. Bake on the middle shelf at 200 °C for 40 minutes. Remove from the oven, cover with a cloth and allow to sweat for a few seconds. Turn out onto a wire rack and gloss the tops and sides with butter. Wrap in cloths and leave to sweat in an upright position to let the steam escape.

Makes 2 large loaves and 1 small loaf

QUICK ONION BREAD

This loaf won't last long – your family will polish it off in no time!

2 eggs, beaten
30 ml (2 tbsp) condensed milk
15 ml (1 tbsp) oil
5 x 250 ml (5 cups) cake flour
20 ml (1½ tbsp) self-raising flour
15 g (1 tbsp) instant dry yeast
7.5 ml (1½ tsp) medium-coarse salt
125 ml (½ cup) onion slices, fried in
10 ml (2 tsp) oil
375 ml (1½ cups) boiling water

Combine the eggs, condensed milk and oil, mix well and set aside. Mix the flours, yeast and salt together. Add the fried onions, water, slightly cooled, and the egg and condensed milk mixture. Make into a dough using your fingers and the heel of your hands. Transfer the dough to a greased bread pan and place in an airtight plastic bag. Cover with a cloth and leave in a warm place for about 25–30 minutes. Preheat the oven to 200 °C. Remove the dough from the plastic bag and bake the bread on the middle shelf of the oven for 40 minutes – the bread will rise quickly. Remove from the oven and allow to stand for 2 minutes. Turn out and gloss the sides and tops of the loaves with a little butter or margarine. Wrap in a cloth and leave to sweat – this will ensure a soft crust.

Makes 2 medium loaves, or 1 large and 1 small loaf

Quick Onion Bread and Sunflower and Sesame Seed Loaf (page 140)

MOSBROOD

Grape bread is a treat from the old days and must be made in summer when grapes are in season.

1 kg hanepoot grapes, peeled and pitted
125 g (½ cup) butter or margarine
60 ml (¼ cup) oil
10 x 250 ml (10 cups) white bread flour
4 x 250 ml (4 cups) self-raising flour
60 ml (¼ cup) white sugar
10 ml (2 tsp) aniseed
10 ml (2 tsp) medium-coarse salt
1 egg, beaten
10 ml (2 tsp) instant dry yeast

Place the grapes in a large bowl and mash roughly to form a pulp. Cover the bowl with plastic and leave to stand overnight. Heat the pulp slowly in a pot until lukewarm before using. Place the grape pulp, butter and oil in a mixing bowl. Combine all the dry ingredients, add to bowl and knead to form a dough. Allow to rise for 2 hours, then punch down very lightly. Turn out onto a floured surface and divide the dough in half. Place in 2 well-greased baking pans. Preheat the oven to 200 °C and bake on the middle shelf for 40 minutes. Remove the loaves from the oven, gloss the tops and sides with a little butter or margarine, and wrap in dry cloths to sweat for a few minutes. Serve with your favourite jam and filter coffee.
Makes 2 loaves

LIGHT BROWN ROLLS

Ideal for a picnic or with a salad.

500 ml (2 cups) white cake flour
250 ml (1 cup) brown bread meal
250 ml (1 cup) self-raising flour
10 ml (2 tsp) instant dry yeast
15 ml (1 tbsp) butter
2.5 ml (½ tsp) medium-coarse salt
10 ml (2 tsp) oil
375 ml (1½ cups) warm water
1 egg, beaten

Sift the dry ingredients together in a large bowl. Add the remaining ingredients and knead to form a dough. Turn out onto a floured surface and form the dough into a sausage shape. Cut 2 cm lengths off with a knife, roll into balls and place, slightly apart, on a well-greased baking tray. Preheat the oven to 180 °C. Cover the baking tray with plastic and leave the dough to rise and double in size for 30 minutes. Remove the plastic and bake on the middle shelf of the oven for 25 minutes. Remove the rolls from the oven and gloss the tops with a little butter. Wrap in cloths and leave to sweat for a few minutes.
Makes 24 rolls

CHEESE AND PARSLEY BREAD

My granny used to make this round, savoury loaf – treat your family to it.

750 ml (3 cups) cake flour
125 ml (½ cup) self-raising flour
7.5 ml (1½ tsp) medium-coarse salt
10 g (2 tsp) instant dry yeast
10 ml (2 tsp) sugar
30 ml (2 tbsp) melted butter
100 g (½ cup) grated Parmesan or Cheddar cheese
1 large egg, beaten
60 ml (¼ cup) chopped parsley
375 ml (1½ cups) warm milk

Combine all the dry ingredients in a large mixing bowl. Add the remaining ingredients to form a dough and knead well, working lightly. Leave to rise until double in size, then punch down and turn out onto a floured surface. Make a round loaf and transfer it to a well-greased, deep, round baking pan. Oil a piece of plastic, cover the pan and leave to stand in a warm spot for about 30 minutes. Preheat the oven to 200 °C. Remove the plastic and bake the bread on the middle shelf for 30 minutes, then turn out onto a wire rack and gloss the top and sides with a little butter or margarine. Wrap in a cloth and leave to sweat for a few minutes – the cloth helps to keep the crust soft.
Makes 1 loaf

MOSBOLLETJIES

Mosbolletjies, or aniseed balls, are delicious served with white cheese and coffee. Bits of orange or lemon peel can be added to the dough.

125 g (½ cup) butter
4 x 250 ml (4 cups) self-raising flour
125 ml (½ cup) cake flour
2 eggs, beaten
10 g (2 tsp) yeast diluted with
2.5 ml (½ tsp) sugar and
15 ml (1 tbsp) lukewarm water
5 ml (1 tsp) aniseed
30 ml (2 tbsp) castor sugar
2.5 ml (½ tsp) salt
185 ml (¾ cup) warm milk
10 ml (2 tsp) oil

Rub the butter lightly into the sifted flours using your fingers and then add the eggs. Add the diluted yeast, aniseed, sugar, salt, milk and oil and blend lightly – do not knead. The dough must be loose, soft and moist. Break the dough into balls of a similar size to scones, place on a greased baking sheet and bake for 20 minutes at 180 °C or until golden brown. Turn out onto a wire rack and brush with sugar water. Cover with a cloth and leave to sweat for a few minutes.

Makes 12–14 balls

Mosbolletjies

SUNFLOWER AND SESAME SEED LOAF

A sure winner!

4 x 250 ml (4 cups) Nutty
Wheat Flour
60 ml (¼ cup) digestive bran
60 ml (¼ cup) self-raising flour
5 ml (1 tsp) bicarbonate of soda
5 ml (1 tsp) medium-coarse salt
60 ml (¼ cup) sesame seeds
60 ml (¼ cup) sunflower seeds
500 ml (2 cups) stirred
Bulgarian yoghurt
10 ml (2 tsp) treacle (see page 124)
30 ml (2 tbsp) honey or golden syrup
1 egg, beaten, mixed with 125 ml
(½ cup) milk and 15 ml (1 tbsp) oil

In a large mixing bowl, mix the dry ingredients together with a wooden spoon and then add the yoghurt. Blend well, then add the treacle and honey and milk mixture, mixing thoroughly. Grease a sandwich loaf baking pan and line the bottom with greaseproof paper. Pour the mixture into the pan, cover with plastic and leave to prove for about 10 minutes. Preheat the oven to 180 °C. Remove the plastic and bake on the middle shelf of the oven for about 1 hour. Remove from the pan, gloss the top and sides with a little soft butter or margarine, wrap in a cloth and leave to sweat standing in a vertical position – this lets the steam escape from beneath the bread.
Makes 1 loaf

NOTE: Line bread pans with greaseproof paper or brown paper. To aid the bread rising, wrap in an airtight plastic bag and a thick cloth.

POTATO FRITTERS

Use 500 g peeled sweet potatoes instead of potatoes, if preferred. Cut them into chips which will stick out of the fritters when cooked, giving them an uneven shape.

2 large potatoes, peeled and halved
60 g (¼ cup) butter, melted
250 ml (1 cup) cake flour
2.5 ml (½ tsp) baking powder
1 egg, beaten
a pinch ground nutmeg
60 ml (¼ cup) cold milk
250 ml (1 cup) oil
cinnamon sugar for dusting

Cook the potatoes and mash with the butter. Add the remaining ingredients, except the oil and cinnamon sugar, to form a pliable batter. Heat the oil in a large, shallow pan – there must be enough oil to generously cover the bottom of the pan. Dip a dessertspoon into the hot oil, then into the batter, and drop spoonfuls of batter into the oil. Fry until golden brown. Remove with a slotted spoon, roll in the cinnamon sugar and serve hot.
Makes about 20 small or 14 large fritters

PUMPKIN FRITTERS

Also called 'pampoen vetkoekies', they are favourite tea time and TV treats in our family.

Pumpkin Fritters, top, and Sweetcorn Puffs (page 143)

**500 g pumpkin, peeled, cooked,
  drained and pulped
250 ml (1 cup) cake flour
5 ml (1 tsp) baking powder
1 egg, beaten
a pinch of salt
30 ml (2 tbsp) melted butter
a pinch of ground nutmeg
60 ml (¼ cup) milk
375 ml (1½ cups) oil
cinnamon sugar for dusting**

Mix all the ingredients together, except the oil and cinnamon sugar, to form a stiffish batter. Heat the oil in heavy-based frying pan on medium-high, using only enough to generously cover the bottom of the pan. Dip a dessertspoon into the oil, then into the batter, and drop spoonfuls of batter into the pan. Fry until golden brown on both sides. Lift out with a slotted spoon or an egg lifter and drain on greaseproof or brown paper. Serve hot, dusted with cinnamon sugar.
Makes about 20 small or 14 large fritters

NOTES:
- 500 g potatoes, mashed with a dash of milk, can be used instead of pumpkin for the Pumpkin Fritters.
- For a delicious variation, substitute well-drained whole-kernel corn for rice in the Rice Fritters (page 143).
- Never peel an orange with a knife. Rather, toss it in boiling water and leave for 10 minutes, then peel it by hand. It makes the orange easier to peel and it won't be bitter.

MALAY ROTI

Roti is the Malay word for unleavened bread, adapted from the Indian recipe, and is often served with curries instead of rice. Use your fingers to break off a piece of roll and scoop up some curry.

750 ml (5 cups) cake flour
a pinch baking powder
7.5 ml (1½ tsp) medium-coarse salt
375 ml (1½ cups) warm water
75 g (5 tbsp) butter, melted
125 ml (½ cup) oil

Mix the flour, baking powder, salt and water together to form a dough. On a floured surface, work the dough until pliable, bringing it together with your fingers. Add a little oil if necessary to make working the dough easier. Roll out and spread with the melted butter. Sprinkle with a little flour and roll up to form a long, thick sausage. Cut it into 5 cm long pieces and stand pieces on their sides, so that the whirls are visible. Roll and turn each piece of dough a few times to form a rough circle, about 20 cm in diameter and as thick as a pancake – it must not be too thin. Cut off any sharp edges with a sharp knife to make it round. Heat a cast-iron pan or heavy-based pan over medium heat and smear with a little oil, about 5 ml (1 tsp). Place a roti in the pan and dab with oil using hard greaseproof paper or butter paper. As it cooks, the roti will rise and bubble slightly. Turn with a palette knife or an egg lifter about four times until it is lightly browned and speckled on both sides. Take freshly cooked roti and crunch gently in your hands to give it a crumpled effect. Transfer to a fairly deep dish and cover with a cloth to allow the roti to sweat – this prevents the edges becoming rough. Continue making rotis until all the dough has been used. If there's a tendency to dryness while frying, dab a little more oil on the roti.

Makes about 7

NOTES:

• Using boiling water instead of warm water will give you a flat roti, similar to pita bread. The warm water makes it flaky.
• TO FREEZE: Layer cooked rotis with greaseproof paper between them. Wrap in foil so that they are airtight, and freeze. Defrost by warming them slowly in a 100 °C oven, steam, covered, over a pot of boiling water, or microwave on 50% for 20–30 seconds per roti.
• For good results, chill your rolling pin in the fridge before using it.

Malay Roti served with Braised Steak Mince (page 43)

PIZZA

Remember to always have peeled and pulped tomatoes as your first layer on the pizza base. See the Notes (below) for filling suggestions.

DOUGH
1 egg, beaten
2.5 ml (½ tsp) salt
500 ml (2 cups) flour
7.5 ml (1½ tsp) baking powder
125 ml (½ cup) warm milk
5 ml (1 tsp) sugar
5 ml (1 tsp) oil
2.5 ml (½ tsp) chilli powder
a pinch dried tarragon
a pinch dried oregano
a pinch dried thyme
5 ml (1 tsp) masala

To make the dough, mix all the ingredients together, except the masala, in a mixing bowl, working until soft and pliable. Roll out the dough on a floured surface and sprinkle with the masala. Grease a pizza pan and line with the dough. Bake blind at 180 °C for 5 minutes on the middle shelf. Remove from the oven. Top it with a filling of your choice. It's best eaten immediately but can be heated in the oven later.
Makes 1 medium pizza

NOTES:
- Various fillings can be used – first spread a layer of tomato pulp over the base, then add your filling and sprinkle grated cheese over if desired. Bake at 180 °C for 20 minutes or until the cheese has melted.
- Tangy pilchard or tuna smoor, flaked chicken cooked with mushrooms and herbs, shrimp and mussel smoor, or fried mince with herbs, onion, mushroom and tomato and a little masala are some of the fillings that may tempt you.

SWEETCORN PUFFS

Another tasty after-dinner or TV snack to serve with coffee.

125 ml (½ cup) cake flour
250 ml (1 cup) self-raising flour
250 ml (1 cup) milk
1 x 410 g tin whole-kernel corn, drained
1 drop butter essence
2.5 ml (½ tsp) salt
30 ml (2 tbsp) butter or margarine, melted
1 egg, beaten
5 ml (1 tsp) baking powder
375 ml (1½ cups) oil
cinnamon sugar for dusting

Sift the flours together and add the milk slowly to form a batter. Mix in the remaining ingredients, except the oil and cinnamon sugar. Heat the oil on medium-high. Dip a tablespoon first into the oil, then into the batter, and drop spoonfuls of batter into the oil. Flip over, then pierce with a fork – if the fork comes out dry, the puffs are done. Remove with a slotted spoon and drain on greaseproof or brown paper. Roll in the cinnamon sugar and serve hot with a choice coffee.
Makes about 20 small or 15 large puffs

RICE FRITTERS

500 ml (2 cups) cooked rice
a pinch ground nutmeg
1 egg, beaten
10 ml (2 tsp) butter, melted
250 ml (1 cup) cake flour
5 ml (1 tsp) baking powder
milk to bind
375 ml (1½ cups) oil
cinnamon sugar for dusting

Blend all the ingredients together, except the oil and cinnamon sugar, to form a stiffish batter, which must be neither too dry nor too wet. Heat the oil in a deep pan on medium-high. Dip a tablespoon into the oil and then into the batter; fry spoonfuls until golden brown on both sides. Lift out with an egg lifter and drain on greaseproof paper. Sprinkle with the cinnamon sugar.
Makes about 20 small or 14 large fritters